THE OFFICIAL
SEX, DRUGS, AND ROCK 'N' ROLL
BOOK OF LISTS

THE OFFICIAL
SEX, DRUGS, AND ROCK 'N' ROLL
BOOK OF LISTS

JUDY MCGUIRE

SOFT SKULL PRESS

First published in 2011 by Backbeat Books

ISBN 978-1-59376-445-6

Illustrations by Cliff Mott
Book design by Kristina Rolander

Soft Skull Press
New York, NY

www.softskull.com

THIS BOOK IS DEDICATED TO MY LUV-UH MAN,
SPYRO PANOUSOPOULOS, WHO HELPED ME THROUGH THIS PROJECT
IN A MILLION DIFFERENT WAYS.

CONTENTS

2. NOT GETTING ANY

3. NAUGHTY BITS

4. WOMEN'S STUDIES

5. GAY STUDIES

6. GIRLS (AND BOYS) ON FILM

7. GROUPIES

8. LOVE AND MARRIAGE

PART TWO: DRUGS

9. THE PRACTICAL DRUG USERS

10. THE DARK SIDE

II. THE LIGHTER SIDE

12. BOOZE

EPILOGUE: WHEN SEX MEETS DRUGS

13. ALL MIXED UP

14. THE HANGOVER

FOREWORD
by Oderus Urungus of Gwar

We love this book, but there is a problem: As far as sex goes, we're not really attracted to human scum. The typical rock 'n' roll groupie is not attractive to us, unless, of course, it is a multiple amputee with a hive of insects for a vagina.

My views on sex are fairly straightforward. But straightforward for a mutated chaos demon-thing such as myself is still pretty fucked up. On many nights there will be hordes of willing sex slaves hanging their tits over the edge of the stage in the desperate hope of being chosen by me, only to have their faces burned off by the corrosive slime of my sputum. My tastes usually bend to the more traditional and ancient ways, like necro-bestial-anal-butt-sex. Currently I am back together with my on-again off-again girlfriend of many years, Pookie the Wonder Dog.

That is not to say that we do not make savage love to our fans—we do. Every Gwar performance is sure to culminate in a seed-letting of tidal proportion. And I will often spend hours after the show hanging around the trash Dumpsters, having sex with whoever wants some, and many who do not. When I release my bloated, bloody load on the upturned faces and bared bosoms of the gibbering masses, you will either die or get pregnant. Gwar sperm will make whatever part of your body it lands on completely child-infested. If it gets on your butthole, you will have a baby out of your ass. I've seen it all, babies crawling out the eyes, the penis, you name it… plus these babies are born addicted to crack! And let's never forget, every time you have sex with Gwar, it's actually incest, because I created you by having sex with apes! The only reason humans exist is because of Gwar. You're all descended from us. If it weren't for our sexual frolicking, the human race wouldn't exist. In short, sex is the entire reason you exist, and its importance cannot be stressed enough!

On to drugs. I am the biggest junkie/crackhead/stoner/violent drunk/drug sponge in the universe. Drugs are great. I do it all, but I love crack the best. People ask me, Why do you love crack so much? With no delay, I respond, What's not to love? It gets you high. Really, *really* high. It tastes great, and whether you eat it or use it as an anal suppository, it's the cat's pajamas. Pot is just boring. It's for pimply-faced, Dungeons and Dragons–playing art-school flunkies who just lost their job at the Hobby Lobby. Plus it smells awful! Alcohol is fun because it drives people into violent rages, so that's okay. Ecstasy? We don't like the hug drug, and we don't like acid either. We do like animal tranquilizers though.

As far as rock 'n' roll goes, we hate all other bands. They all suck. Though that guy from Creed who got drunk as shit and threw up all over the place is okay. And so is the guy with the tattooed chin from Devil Driver. But most rock personalities are just so blah. So I decided to make it easy on myself and only listen to Motörhead.

PREFACE

Sex and drugs go with rock 'n' roll like Sonny goes with Cher or Sanford goes with Son. Elvis the Pelvis gets banned from TV for his naughty swivel and then dies on the john with a gut full of pills while thirty-plus years later Lady Gaga sings about being "born this way" and confesses her love for cocaine to *Rolling Stone* magazine. Though obviously not every rock star is a smack-gobbling ho-bag, drugs and sex brush up against every genre of rock, soul, pop, rhythm 'n' blues, and rap.

Which is why the title of this book is *The* Official *Book of Sex, Drugs, and Rock 'n' Roll Lists*, not *The* Complete *Book of Sex, Drugs, and Rock 'n' Roll Lists*. I make this distinction because the more I dug, the more I found, and the more obvious it became that in order to make this book truly exhaustive and cram every bit rock 'n' roll–fueled druggery and fuckery inside, it would wind up the size of the *Encyclopaedia Britannica*. I mean, let's face it, Pete Doherty alone could fill an entire volume. Jerry Garcia? Several.

So what you're holding is sort of a greatest hits of rock 'n' roll debauchery. There are boobs, bongs, groupies, gonads, venereal diseases, and death. On the downside, even if you roll it up and smoke it, this book won't get you high; but on the bright side, it won't give you herpes.

—Judy McGuire

14 TIPS FOR CLEAN AND SOBER LIVING FROM OZZY OSBOURNE

Though he's better known as the bat-biting Prince of Darkness, Ozzy Osbourne has a lot of knowledge to share. And share it he does with columns addressing medical and manner issues in *Rolling Stone* and the *Times* of London. Here are some of his best bits of wisdom (and wit).

I. On athlete's foot

I used to cure athlete's foot by pouring cocaine on my toes. They cut the stuff with so much foot powder back then, it was the best treatment you could find if you had an outbreak on the road. The only problem was the price, which was around $3,000 a toe.

2. Heartburn

I'd wake at 2 a.m. with a burning sensation on my chest. I cured it by not going to sleep with a lit cigarette in my hand anymore.

3. Vertigo

I thought I had vertigo…I went to the doctor, and he said, "Mr. Osbourne, the problem—as far as I can tell—is simply that you're very, very drunk…."

4. Convincing your young son to quit smoking

Put your son off cigarettes by making him ill. Throw some fag ash on his cornflakes. With any luck, that'll do the trick.

5. On antidepressants

Antidepressants are fabulous things…but they'll play havoc with your meat and two veg. I've been taking them for years and what I've found is, I can do everything except the after-show fireworks. So I just end up pumping away on top of Sharon like a road drill all night.

6. On a daughter's nose job request

People get birthmarks and other harmless things removed because of the way they look. It's no different with a giant conk. Buy her the nose job.

7. On cheapness

If your friends are saying they're offended by your behavior, chances are you're tighter than Elvis Presley's spandex. So it can't hurt to dig deep for a while, just to prove them wrong.

8. On asking a girlfriend to get a boob job

Under no circumstances bring this up with your girlfriend. If I made this suggestion to Sharon, the Osbourne crown jewels would end up halfway up my esophagus.

9. On impotence

Calm down, don't drink beforehand, and cut out the five-knuckle shuffles.

10. On curing a filthy belly button

After you've cleaned out the fluff, try keeping a pack of mints in there or something. That should stop debris building up.

11. On male pedicures

I'm the Prince of Darkness and I've had more pedicures than hot dinners.

12. On dealing with your wife's period

If there are four words a married man should never say to his wife—especially during an argument—they are "time of the month." It's the atomic-bomb option, and the bomb's only ever gonna land in one place: on your own head.

13. On watching porn

I watch 'em on the road from time to time because it's better than picking up some groupie and having my love spuds turn green (not to mention I'm a happily married man).

14. On taking LSD

I remember once walking into a field in Staffordshire when I was high as a kite and having a long conversation with a cow. After a while, the cow turned to another cow and said: "Bugger me, that bloke can talk."

Compiled from Ozzy's advice columns in *Rolling Stone* and the *Sunday Times* of London.

PART ONE: SEX

BUMPIN' UGLIES

1

14 SEXUAL INSIGHTS AND LOVEMAKING TECHNIQUE TIPS FROM MÖTLEY CRÜE

Music writer Mick Wall once described the Crüe as making Led Zeppelin "look like pussycats." The band has sold millions of records, snorted, smoked, and shot up hundreds of pounds of drugs, and fucked more women than most men will even see fully clothed over their entire lifetimes. As bassist Nikki Sixx so wisely put it, "You may as well learn about sex from Mötley Crüe [rather] than your parents—it's a lot more fun."

DR. VINCE NEIL, LEAD SINGER

1. "We were always fucking other chicks at the studio and backstage…. We would take Tommy's van to a restaurant called Noggles to buy these egg burritos and then rub them on our crotches to cover the smell of the girls we had just fucked…. [W]e never thought about going into the restroom and just washing our dicks." (*Hustler*)

2. "Well, sometimes I just want to get back on the tour bus and watch a little *Judge Judy*. Just relax with a peanut butter and jelly sandwich and some *Judge Judy* and that's it, man. Those are some good times." (*Vanity Fair*, Nov. 27, 2009)

3. "When we were really hard up, Nikki and I would date girls who worked in grocery stores just for the free food. But we always bought our own booze. It was a matter of pride." (*The Dirt*)

DR. TOMMY LEE, DRUMMER/SWORDSMAN

4. "My favorite thing to do when I'm in the southland is to pull my girl's lips all the way back so that her little Gummi Bear just pops out at me. Dude, I love Gummi Bears!" (*Tommyland*)

5. "Let's not forget to drink our pineapple juice every morning either, fellas. A glass a day will do ya—an hour before you get it on is even better. It'll make your cum sweet and your girl will definitely love you for that. That's one for you, ladies!" (*Tommyland*)

6. On sobriety: "You f*ck a lot more too man, I'm digging that.... [S]ometimes I would start hittin' it at noon with a vodka lemonade so by two in morning you're just tired and the last thing you want is to get fucking crazy. So I'm just a lot clearer, fucking hornier, so it's a good thing." (AskMen.com)

7. "We know from SeaWorld's own director of safety (as well as videos on the web) that the way you get his sperm is by having someone get into the pool and masturbate him with a cow's vagina filled with hot water.... [E]ven in my wildest days with Mötley Crüe, I never could've imagined something so sick and twisted."(From an outraged letter to SeaWorld regarding their manual stimulation of Tilikum the killer whale)

DR. NIKKI SIXX, BASSIST

8. METAL SLUDGE: If you could be a tampon for a celebrity, who would you choose?

   NIKKI: Sophia Loren (Metal Sludge)

9. "As I get older my eyesight's going bad. I don't know what I'm in for until they come backstage and they're very large with missing teeth. You go to the bigger cities and you get the silicone breasts, the bleach blonde hair and the super-skinny tight pants, which is attractive…until they talk." (ClashMusic.com)

10. "It's like a light switch. I'm the only Italian under one inch…. You're either a shower or a grower—right? Some guys just pull it out and you're like 'woah' and then it only grows about a half inch. I'm a grower." (Interview with Howard Stern)

11. "Sex to me was always about conquest. Girls were a form of entertainment, nothing more, and when heroin came along, it blew them away." (*The Heroin Diaries: A Year in the Life of a Shattered Rock Star*)

12. "Pussy's so boring to me after I've had it—drugs never got boring for me." (*When Rock Ruled the World*, documentary series on BBC)

DR. MICK MARS, GUITARIST

13. Sexy crafts project: "The banner behind us was Nikki or Tommy's unwashed bedsheet, which still had bloodstains on it from girls they had slept with." (*The Dirt*)

14. "I guess it's like the Rolling Stones and shit. They're all wrinkled up, and they're still walking around with these beautiful girls around them all the time. And these girls that are still coming to our shows aren't the daughters anymore. In fact, they're bringing their daughters now!" (Associated Content)

HONORABLE MENTION FROM THE PEANUT GALLERY (BECAUSE IT'S GOOD ADVICE)

DR. DONNA D'ERRICO, THEN-WIFE OF NIKKI SIXX

"Don't try to reenact a porn movie you saw and start smackin' their asses, thinking you are all studly. It's not a turn-on. What you should do is make sure you know what you're doing while performing cunnilingus. There is nothing worse than a speedy tongue guy. Make sure you're on the right spot and ask questions. Just don't think you're the cunnilingus god while you're down there, and she's up there in hell." (*Hustler*)

NOTHIN' FANCY—JUST 16 BANDS PAYING TRIBUTE TO SEXY TIMES

1. The Bumpin' Uglies
2. Buster Hymen and the Penetrators
3. Cherry Poppin' Daddies
4. Crucifucks
5. Doggy Style
6. The F.U.'s
7. Human Sexual Response
8. Sarcastic Orgasm
9. Sex Beat
10. Sex Mob
11. Sex Rat
12. Sic Fucks
13. Sloppy Seconds
14. Stains
15. Tokyo Sex Destruction
16. Torsofuck

PAT KIERNAN'S AND CAITLIN DREXLER'S 10 THINLY VEILED SEX SONGS

Not a lot of people can say a Captain and Tennille song led to an epiphany.

I've been complaining about how most of the chart-topping music this summer is unsuitable for family consumption. What father wants to hear his daughter and her friends singing, "Give it to me, baby like boom boom boom!" into their hairbrushes?

But then I walked into a store a week ago and heard Captain and Tennille on the radio. And as I listened closely to the lyrics of "Do It to Me One More Time," I realized my complaint about raunchy song lyrics isn't just a new kids-these-days problem. Is Tennille's plea any more subtle than Rihanna's "Rude Boy" lyrics? Standing in that store, there didn't seem to be anything subtle about it.

Immediately, I started diving into my mental music catalog to come up with other titles that are innocently played on easy-listening radio stations but are really just thinly veiled songs about sex. Here, "Pat's Papers" producer Caitlin Drexler and I present our walk down musical memory lane.

Below are ten classic songs about sex—you just might not have realized it. The 1980s seemed to be the nexus of the double entendre so we didn't stray too far from the decade when making our selections. Somehow the songs don't sound so bad when the lyrics are wrapped up in the music. But a closer examination of some of these gems might have you thinking twice before singing along in the bank lobby.

10. "Physical," Olivia Newton John
Thinly veiled lyric: "There's nothing left to talk about / Unless it's horizontally."
Most explicit lyric: "You gotta know that you're bringin' out / The animal in me."

9. "Little Red Corvette," Prince
Thinly veiled lyric: "'Cause you had a pocket full of horses / Trojan and some of them used."
Most explicit lyric: "I'm gonna try to tame your little red love machine."

8. "Nobody Does It Better," Carly Simon
Thinly veiled lyric: "But like Heaven above me, the spy who loved me / Is keeping all my secrets safe tonight."
Most explicit lyric: "Nobody does it quite the way you do / Why'd you have to be so good?"

7. "Relax," Frankie Goes to Hollywood

Thinly veiled lyric: "Come / But shoot it in the right direction / Make makin' it your intention."
Most explicit lyric: "Relax, don't do it / When you want to suck, do it."

6. "She Bop," Cyndi Lauper

Thinly veiled lyric: "They say I better stop or I'll go blind."
Most explicit lyric: "Huh, yea, I want to go south and get me some more."

5. "I'm Your Gun," Alice Cooper

Thinly veiled lyric: "You be the target on the bed / I'll be shooting hot lead."
Most explicit lyric: "Pull my trigger, I get bigger / Then I'm lots of fun / I'm your gun."

4. "Natural Woman," Aretha Franklin

Thinly veiled lyric: "You make me feel like a natural woman."
Most explicit lyric: "You make me feel so good inside."

3. "Afternoon Delight," Starland Vocal Band

Thinly veiled lyric: "And I think I might try nibbling a little afternoon delight."
Most explicit lyric: "Rubbin' sticks and stones together makes the sparks ignite / And the thought of rubbin' you is getting so exciting."

2. "One More Time," Captain and Tennille

Thinly veiled lyric: "Pass that by me one more time / Once is never enough for my heart to hear."
Most explicit lyric: "Do that to me one more time / Once is never enough with a man like you."

I. "Sledgehammer," Peter Gabriel

Thinly veiled lyric: "Open up your fruit cage / Where the fruit is as sweet as can be."
Most explicit lyric: "You could have a big dipper / Going up and down, all around the bends."

Pat Kiernan is the anchor of the morning news program on NY1 News in New York City. He's known to national audiences for his work as host of several game shows, including *World*

Series of Pop Culture. Pat came to New York in 1996 from his native Canada and quickly became an essential part of city's morning routine.

Caitlin Drexler is the producer of "Pat's Papers," the cross-country equivalent of the NYC-focused "In the Papers" segment Pat prepares each morning for NY1. A graduate of the CUNY Graduate School of Journalism, she wakes up at the crack of dawn every morning to read dozens of newspapers in search of the country's best stories.

JUDY MCGUIRE LISTS 8 REASONS YOU SHOULDN'T LISTEN TO LYRICS FOR HELP WITH YOUR LOVE LIFE (AND ONE REASON WHY YOU SHOULD)

Musicians may have more sex than your average bear, but as the bad advice covered in these lyrics show, they may not always know what they're talking about. The following are some egregious examples of misguided advice.

1. Bad advice: "Pour some sugar on me." ("Pour Some Sugar on Me," Def Leppard)

Correction: When you introduce overly sugary products into your lovemaking routine, you're asking for trouble. The vadge has a very precise pH balance and anything that knocks it out of whack can cause a yeast or bacterial infection.

2. Bad advice: "Just one touch and I erupt." ("Sexy Love," Ne-Yo)

Correction: Though Ne-Yo brags that he covers her "like a volcano" after just one brush of the hand, the reality is that premature ejaculation can be a very frustrating thing for the ladies. If you're quick on the trigger like Ne-Yo, I'd quit advertising it and instead advise taking care of business solo earlier in the day to get it out of your system. Nobody likes a two-pump chump.

3. Bad advice: "I'ma get, get, get, get, you drunk / Get you love drunk off my hump." ("My Humps," Black Eyed Peas)

Correction: I'll admit that Fergie has some yummy-looking lady lumps, but alcohol is not an acceptable accompaniment to foreplay. Judgment gets impaired, condoms can be discarded…all sorts of trouble can erupt.

4. Bad advice: "Love slipped from my lips, dripped down my chin and landed in his lap . ." ("Love Rain," Jill Scott)

Correction: Whether you choose to spit or swallow, there's no excuse for sloppy semen handling. Keep a tissue nearby if you're the former and work on that gag reflex if the latter is your method of choice.

5. Bad advice: "I'll let you whip me if I misbehave." ("Sexy Back," Justin Timberlake)

Correction: You'll *let* me whip you? What kind of bottom are you, J.T.? I'll tell you when you misbehave and I'll decide what kind of punishment is called for. Few things are more annoying than an uppity sub.

6. Bad advice: "Blowing and hoeing and covered in mud." ("Sex Cow," Gwar)

Correction: Again, mud is a breeding ground for bacteria.

7. Bad advice: "I'll give you head . till your love is red." ("Head," Prince)

Correction: Though Prince is reportedly heterosexual, it doesn't matter which gender's genitalia you're entertaining with your tongue in this context. While yes, it's great when the organ gets engorged with blood, Prince follows this line with "love you till you're dead," which is less appetizing and makes his intentions seem somewhat sinister.

8. Bad advice: "I wanna fuck you like an animal." ("Closer," Nine Inch Nails)

Correction: Actually, this depends on which animal. Doggy-style, fine. Like a pig, with its corkscrew-shaped wang? No thanks. Also, if you're donkey-dicked, make sure you use lube.

HONORABLE MENTION

Good advice: "If you want my body and you think I'm sexy / Come on sugar let me know." ("Do Ya Think I'm Sexy?," Rod Stewart)
Rod's right—why play games?

Judy McGuire is the author of this book and has been writing a sex and love column called "Dategirl" for the *Seattle Weekly* for more than ten years now. You can find her at www.dategirl.net.

100 SONGS ABOUT FUCKING

I. "Gimme! Gimme! Gimme!," Abba
Sure, Abba may have looked and sounded as pure as driven snow, but that doesn't mean they didn't have needs. Needs that they expressed in this demanding little ditty.

2. "You Shook Me All Night Long," AC/DC
If you haven't dry-humped to this song at least once in your life, you're missing out.

3. "Love in an Elevator," Aerosmith
"Livin' it up while I'm goin' down" is all about sex on the job.

4. "I Want to Fuck You," Akon
It's difficult to decipher exactly what Akon is getting at in this extremely nuanced number, but it seems to be something involving mashing genitalia.

5. "Come Again," the Au Pairs
Great song about a boring fingerbang: "Yes, it was nice / Yes, we should go to sleep now."

6. "I Want You (She's So Heavy)," Beatles

These mop-tops were possibly the least sexy band of all time, but this is a song about yearning for a fat chick. (Kidding—they mean heavy in the philosophical sense. I think.)

7. "Shut Up and Fuck," Betty Blowtorch

These ladies knew what they wanted: "I don't want you to be mine / I just wanna sixty-nine."

8. "Kangaroo," Big Star

If "I want you, like a kangaroo" isn't sexy, what is?

9. "Nick the Stripper," Birthday Party

Young Nick Cave. Naked. Enough said.

10. "Nonstoperotik," Black Francis

The Pixies front man "cannot hide." He wants "to be inside."

11. "La Menage," Black Sheep

There's so much goodness to parse (including something about administering DIY hysterectomies), but one of the funnier lines is "If sexy were a virus, then you have a disease."

12. "The Bad Touch," Bloodhound Gang

Not all songs about sex are arousing, as Bloodhound Gang proves as they implore you to "do it like they do on the Discovery Channel."

13. "Girls and Boys," Blur

The message behind this catchy tune is it doesn't matter *who* you love, it's *that* you love.

14. "Get Up (Feel like a Sex Machine)," James Brown

More than a sex soundtrack, this jumping anthem is much more of a get-in-the-mood song.

15. "Get on Top," Tim Buckley

While a little instructional can be hot, being told, "Well, like a bitch dog in heat, we had those bed springs a-squeakin' all day long," is somewhat less so.

16. "Train Kept a Rollin'," Johnny Burnette and the Rock and Roll Trio

Burnette and his band made the first rock recording of this jump blues song, which was later covered/reinvented by the Yardbirds, Led Zep, Dread Zep, Jeff Beck, Aerosmith, Shakin' Stevens and the Sunsets, Alex Chilton, Metallica, Hanoi Rocks, Twisted Sister, and others.

17. "Do That to Me One More Time," Captain and Tennille

Q: Who knew there was a stud lurking beneath that captain's hat?
A: Tennille

18. "Slip Away," Clarence Carter

Clarence Carter defined the sexy song and this is but one of many.

19. "I Want to Sex You Up," Color Me Badd

The extra *d* is for "extra-douchey."

20. "Hypno Sex Ray," the Cramps

If you were lucky enough to have ever seen a Cramps show, you'd know that everything they did was about sex. But in this one, Lux yowls, "That girl gyration makes my gong go ding!"

21. "Harder, Better, Faster, Stronger," Daft Punk

Not a particularly steamy beat, but good advice, nonetheless.

22. "Say My Name," Destiny's Child

Beyoncé and Co. are begging you to say their name in the bedroom. Not in the hallway or the kitchen—the bedroom.

23. "Come On, Eileen," Dexys Midnight Runners

A perfect example of the importance of correct comma usage. There's not semen spattered *on* Eileen; Kevin Rowland is simply trying to convince Eileen to do him.

24. "Do You See My Love (for You Growing)," Dirtbombs

Unclear whether "love" is a euphemism for something else that's getting bigger.

25. "Hungry like the Wolf," Duran Duran

Hungry for your love! Ah-wooooo!

26. "Wake Up and Make Love With Me," Ian Dury and the Blockheads

What Dury lacked in sex appeal, he more than made up for in charisma and charm.

27. "Lay Lady Lay," Bob Dylan

Back before he turned into a croaker, Dylan was a bit of a crooner.

28. "Stutter," Elastica

Not all sex is good sex, as this infectious ode to whiskey dick makes clear.

29. "Stay with Me," the Faces

The original one-night-stand song, with the caddish Rod promising to kick her out the door if she's still there in the morning.

30. "Feel like Makin' Love," Roberta Flack

Your grandparents probably had sex to this song. Just sayin'.

31. "Business Time," Flight of the Conchords

"You know when I'm down to my socks it's time for business—that's why they're called 'business socks.'"

32. "Urgent," Foreigner

"Your desire is insane. / You can't stop, until you do it again," sang Lou Gramm of his horny minx.

33. "Promiscuous," Nelly Furtado with Timbaland

Nelly turned down $500k to pose nekkid in *Playboy*, which sounds kinda prudish, not promiscuous.

34. "Sledgehammer," Peter Gabriel

In addition to "sledgehammer" being a euphemism for Gabriel's member, Peter also wrote that he wanted to be the "honeybee" in "your "fruit cage."

35. "Je T'Aime...Moi Non Plus," Serge Gainsbourg and Jane Birkin

Even if you don't understand the lingo, all the moaning and groaning makes it clear what this song is about.

36. "Let's Get It On," Marvin Gaye

This played right after the Roberta Flack song on your grandparents' Soundtrack o' Sex.

37. "Ooh La La," Goldfrapp
Sex with a side of glitter.

38. "Susie Q," Dale Hawkins
Everyone from Linda McCartney to Phish to the Rolling Stones covered this ode to a sassy girl named Susie.

39. "Fire," Jimi Hendrix
Jimi was sex on a stick, and if there was any question about that, this song cemented his rep.

40. "Boom Boom," John Lee Hooker
This song is listed as one of the Rock and Roll Hall of Fame's 500 songs that shaped rock 'n' roll. The sexiest lines in this song don't make any sense when you read them, but it's all in the intonation: "*A-haw haw haw haw.*"

41. "You Sexy Thing," Hot Chocolate
Because it's been featured in dozens of films, this is the only song ever to enter the British charts in three different decades—the '70s, the '80s, and the '90s.

42. "Wicked Game," Chris Isaak
This song is a panty-moistener even without the sultry Herb Ritts–directed video, featuring barely clad Danish supermodel Helena Christensen cavorting on the beach with the handsome Isaak.

43. "Between the Sheets," the Isley Brothers
One guess as to what this Isley is doing between the sheets.

44. "Fujiyama Mama," Wanda Jackson
The Queen of Rockabilly would seem to be referencing female ejaculation as she growls, "And when I start erupting ain't nobody gonna make me stop."

45. "I Just Wanna Make Love to You," Etta James
This was the naughty B side to the Obamas' fave song, "At Last."

46. "Press My Button (Ring My Bell)," Lil Johnson
From the blues compilation *Copulation Blues* comes this bawdy masterpiece of female empowerment: "Come on, baby, let's have some fun, just put your hot dog in my bun."

47. "Slow Motion," Juvenile, featuring Soulja Slim

Juvenile implores his lover lady to slow it down, complaining, "My fingers keep slipping, I'm trying to grip that ass."

48. "Milkshake," Kelis

Whatever that "milkshake" might be, it brings all the boys to the yard.

49. "Ignition (Remix)," R. Kelly

Though this song is hot, it quickly cools when you recall who's singing it.

50. "I Feel the Earth Move," Carole King

Also a part of your grandparents' eight-track Sex Cassette, this song is a tribute to the female orgasm. Your *grandmother's* orgasm, to be specific.

51. "Sex on Fire," Kings of Leon

Used as part of the Victoria's Secret Fashion Show soundtrack in 2009. The band claim alternate versions called "Socks on Fire" or "Snatch on Fire."

52. "I Was Made for Lovin' You," Kiss

The tongue says "yes," but Gene Simmons' sex tape will have you saying, "no thanks."

53. "Help Me Make It Through the Night," Kris Kristofferson

Every groupie ever interviewed about him claims Kristofferson is a real mensch, so give him a hand, won't you?

54. "Whole Lotta Love," Led Zeppelin

Robert Plant apparently packed about ten inches of love in his skintight trousers.

55. "Whole Lotta Shakin' Goin' On," Jerry Lee Lewis

Unfortunately, some of that shakin' was goin' on with an underage cousin.

56. "Rough Sex," Lords of Acid

LoA are pretty clear about what they're looking for here: "pure sex, deep sex, hard sex, rough sex—go!"

57. "Justify My Love," Madonna

Most of Madge's music is sexually oriented, but since this video was banned from MTV, we're calling it her sexxxiest.

58. "Electric Feel," MGMT
Ever feel buzzed from love? Yeah, well, this is about that.

59. "I Want Your Sex," George Michael
And George is prepared to seek out that sex in a public lavatory.

60. "A Case of You," Joni Mitchell
In this heartfelt song, Joni talks about drinking "a case of you."

61. "In the Bush," Musique
This studio project by producer Patrick Adams recalls a sweeter time when women still had pubes: "Push, push, in the bush!"

62. "You Can Leave Your Hat On," Randy Newman
The Tom Jones and Joe Cocker versions are better known, but this one is the best.

63. "Closer," Nine Inch Nails
Trent wants to fuck you like an animal.

64. "AA XXX," Peaches
In this dirty ditty, this bossy broad promises that if you behave, you'll be "taking a bite out of the Peach tonight."

65. "Turn Off the Lights," Teddy Pendergrass
Teddy makes dirty clean, suggesting, "Let's take a shower, shower together, yeah."

66. "Flower," Liz Phair
In this, the delightfully philthy Phair promises, "I'll fuck you till your dick is blue." Ouchie.

67. "In the Midnight Hour," Wilson Pickett
This subtly sexy song was covered by the Grateful Dead, Martha Reeves and the Vandellas, Echo and the Bunnymen, and even Johnny Thunders.

68. "Good Hard Fuckin'," Larry Pierce
Downsized former autoworker Pierce has made a career out of writing and performing filthy country songs, but this one is a fave of Howard Stern's, thus its place on our list.

69. "Little Red Corvette," Prince

Before Prince found the Lord, he was a fan of the fuckery. There were many to choose from, but this is one of his best.

70. "Baby Wants to Ride," Jamie Principle

The Chicago-born house music pioneer made a nine-minute "sex mix" of this song, which includes the lyrics "I want to fuck you all night long."

71. "Skin on Skin," Queens of the Stone Age

Who says stoner rock can't be sexy? Josh Homme proves it as he howls, "I hear you comin', ooh, aaaah, baby."

72. "Go All the Way," Raspberries

Because of its naughty nature, this song was originally banned by the uptight BBC.

73. "(Love Is like a) Heat Wave," Martha Reeves and the Vandellas

Martha started off as a secretary at Motown and eventually wound up as a Detroit councilwoman. In 2009 she quit politics and hit the road again, saying she wasn't cut out for a political life because you "have to be dishonest."

74. "I'm Too Sexy," Right Said Fred

For a brief moment in the early '90s this British duo was "so sexy it hurts."

75. "Inside My Love," Minnie Riperton

Comedienne Maya Rudolph's mom was a five-and-a-half-octave singer best known for her hit "Lovin' You." But it's this song, where she implored her lover to "come inside me," that wound up banned by several radio stations.

76. "Let's Spend the Night Together," Rolling Stones

There's no shortage of sexy Stones songs, but this one is one of their finest.

77. "Never Say Never," Romeo Void

New wave bands were superior to punk rock in one way—they sang about sex, not politics.

78. "Push It," Salt-N-Pepa

Sexy and sweet at the same time.

79. "Hold On, I'm Comin'," Sam and Dave
Not sure whether it's Sam or Dave who's comin', but hold on.

80. "Some Velvet Morning," Nancy Sinatra and Lee Hazlewood
Lady teaches man about sex.

81. "I'm On Fire," Bruce Springsteen
Better known for his tributes to the working man, Bruce shows his bonerific side on this one.

82. "Tonight's the Night," Rod Stewart
Sex is a frequent topic for Rod the Mod, but this 1976 hit is his best and features his gorgeous-blonde-of-the-moment Britt Ekland whispering sweet nothings.

83. "Afternoon Delight," Starland Vocal Band
An ode to the nooner.

84. "Love to Love You Baby," Donna Summer
It's a dark day when a disco queen finds the Lord and forsakes her slutty roots, which is exactly what Summer did for twenty-five years. Later, though, she began performing a newly arranged (and presumably cleaned-up) version of the song.

85. "A Screw," Swans
Sasha Grey is a Swans fan. That is all.

86. "Pillow Talk," Sylvia
The '70s were a big time for simulated orgasms in song. Sylvia's hit was originally intended for Al Green, but he turned it down because it went against his religious beliefs.

87. "Get It On," T. Rex
Bang a gong.

88. "I Ain't Gonna Let Nobody Steal My Jelly Roll," Taj Mahal
"Jelly Roll" is one of those rare, non-gender-specific terms for genitalia. Thus when Taj is talking about "his," he's either worried that someone's going to make off with his penis, or—more likely—steal his woman (and her vagina).

89. "Fuck Her Gently," Tenacious D
Jack Black and Kyle Gass wrote and performed this tender tribute to lovemaking.

90. "Hound Dog," Big Mama Thornton
Big Mama recorded the original version of this Leiber and Stoller classic, which was later made famous by Elvis.

91. "Wild Thing," Tone Loc
Best line in a very funny song: "Couldn't get her off my jock, she was like static cling."

92. "Red Light Special," TLC
Lisa "Left Eye" Lopes famously wore a condom over her left eye to illustrate the group's safety-first stance.

93. "Me So Horny," 2 Live Crew
Luther Campbell and Crew were arrested, protested against, and enjoyed a great deal of success because of this filthy little song.

94. "Shake, Rattle and Roll," Big Joe Turner
Bill Haley neutered Turner's original by cutting the line "You make me roll my eyes, baby, make me grit my teeth."

95. "Desire," U2
Comparing his sexual yearning to drug addiction and an illness, Bono makes it clear this song is about a boner.

96. "Ain't Talkin' 'Bout Love," Van Halen
Nope, Dave is talkin' 'bout groupie sex. BTW, according to über-groupie "Sweet" Connie Hamzy, drummer Alex was the best in bed.

97. "You Can Ring My Bell," Anita Ward
Bell = Clitoris. Ring it.

98. "Fuck like a Beast", W.A.S.P.
Singer Blackie Lawless is most famous for wearing a circular-saw codpiece and throwing meat out at the audience.

99. "I'm Gonna Love You Just a Little More Baby," Barry White

Barry White, is there anything you sing that doesn't sound like you're about to get down?

100. "Squeeze Box," the Who

Unlike the myriad blatant "do me" songs that pepper this list, this is just as filthy using only double entendre.

AMANDA HESS'S TOP 10 RAP SEX EUPHEMISMS

Talking about having sex is healthy. But with radio censors intent on bleeping out the most explicitly offensive material, what's Lil Wayne to do when he wants to write an entire song about a woman performing oral sex on him? Invent a bizarre euphemism for fun and profit. Below, the top ten euphemisms for sex made famous in rap songs.

10. Lollipop

Defining moment: Lil Wayne's "Lollipop"
Underlying meaning: Sexual infantilization ahead. According to the Urban Dictionary, "It's basically a cock. As in lick the lollipop. Referring to blowjobs [*sic*]. Lil Wayne made a song called Lollipop about this topic."
See also: 50 Cent's "Candy Shop"

9. Ridin' my pony

Defining moment: Ginuwine's "Pony"
Underlying meaning: Ginuwine's pony, obviously, is his cock. One commenter commends Ginuwine for invoking a diminutive horse as opposed to a more sizable stallion; I'm just impressed he manages to carry the analogy throughout the song. His saddle is waiting, ladies.

8. The nappy dug out

Defining moment: Ice Cube's "Givin' Up the Nappy Dug Out"
Underlying meaning: All this means is vagina, but points for originality.

7. Milkshake

Defining moment: Kelis's "Milkshake"

Underlying meaning: I always assumed "milkshake" stood for "blow job." In the context of the song, that interpretation would have Kelis performing mass outdoor yard blow jobs for all the boys. Kelis had this to say about the true meaning of the frothy drink: "Milkshake is just that thing that makes a woman stand out from everyone else. It's a thing that makes you sensual and warm and maternal. It could be about breasts but I don't have huge tits so you gotta work with what you got."

6. Skeet

Defining moment: Lil Jon's "Get Low"

Underlying meaning: Ejaculating; "to shoot your man juice up on ur bitch."

5. Make it rain

Defining moment: Fat Joe's "Make It Rain"

Underlying meaning: Urban Dictionary identifies two levels of euphemism in this rap standard: "In strip clubs, it is when you throw stacks of money all over women (this is the 'edited' definition)"; "when a man ejaculates all over a woman (this is the 'explicit' definition)." See also: Lil Wayne's "Rain Man (Strip Club Anthem)"

4. Superman that ho

Defining moment: Soulja Boy's "Crank That (Soulja Boy)"

Underlying meaning: Is it not intuitive? "When you cum on a girls back and then stick the sheets to her, so when she wakes up in the morning she has a cape." (UrbanDictionary.com)

3. Wild thing

Defining moment: Tone Loc's "Wild Thing"

Underlying meaning: Dropped in 1989, this song is one of the original examples of hip-hop sex euphemism. Now, "doin' the wild thing" is so intimately associated with having sex that it's hard to believe it was once ambiguous.

2. O.P.P.

Defining moment: Naughty by Nature's "O.P.P."

Underlying meaning: "Other people's property," generally. Throughout the song, "O.P.P." is made to signify both "other people's penis" and "other people's pussy." According to Wikipedia, "when the song asks if the listener is 'down with O.P.P.,' it is asking the listener if he/she is willing to have sexual intercourse with a person who is known to already have a significant other." The enthusiastic call-and-response that

generally accompanies this song suggests that we're all a bunch of cheaters. Or we have no fucking idea what Naughty by Nature is talking about.

1. Doin' it
Defining moment: LL Cool J's "Doin' It"
Underlying meaning: Sex.

Amanda Hess is a Washington, DC–based journalist who specializes in reporting gender and sex issues for TBD.com.

MICHAEL GONZALES'S DIRTY MIND: THE 10 BEST PRINCE TITLES ABOUT SEX

1. "Pink Cashmere"

2. "Get It Up" (recorded by the Time)

3. "Horny Toad"

4. "Head"

5. "G-Spot" (recorded by Jill Jones)

6. "Soft and Wet"

7. "Sugar Walls" (recorded by Sheena Easton)

8. "The Screams of Passion" (recorded by the Family)

9. "Sex Shooter" (recorded by Apollonia 6)

10. "Erotic City"

Michael A. Gonzales calls himself Gonzo, so you do the math. He has written for *New York* magazine, the *Village Voice*, and *High Times*. Back in the 1980s, when he was really drunk and high, he told people he was having an "Axl Rose moment." He currently stays home in Brooklyn.

THE ORAL SUBCATEGORY: 2 BANDS NAMED FOR HUMMERS

1. Machine Gun Fellatio
2. Minnie Pearl Necklace

SOMETIMES YOU NEED A LITTLE HELP: 6 BANDS NAMED AFTER SEX TOYS

1. Arab Strap
2. Ben Wah and the Blue Balls
3. The Fuck Machine
4. Steely Dan
5. Stimulators
6. Vibrators

DUDE, WHERE'S MY V-CARD? 9 ROCKERS (AND ONE ACTOR) TALK ABOUT LOSIN' IT

1. Anthony Kiedis

Kiedis lost his virginity at a scandalously young age to one of his father's girlfriends. *With* dad's blessing.

2. Ozzy Osbourne

You weren't expecting a sweet, romantic tale from the Prince of Darkness were you? Ozzy told a reporter, "I was fifteen when I lost my virginity and I was so randy it felt like my pants were about to explode." (AskMen.com)

3. Katy Perry

Some of us like to hold onto souvenirs. Like Katy Perry, who told her five kajillion Twitter followers, "[My assistant] made me throw away my virginity underwear! NOOOOO!!!!!!! (but then again she said that's not normal to keep those) I AM NOT NORMAL I KNOW!"

4. Lily Allen

In an interview with Nerve.com, Allen revealed how she was relieved of her hymen. "Oh, God! It wasn't very nice. It was with someone from school. It was very messy. I was very young. I don't regret it, but I kind of wish it happened a different way." Allen goes on to share that her worst sexual experience involved a finger-to-anus penetration gone awry. "That wasn't very nice," she said. (Nerve.com, Feb. 6, 2007)

5. Marc Bolan

According to the film *Marc Bolan: 20th Century Boy*, Bolan was only nine when he first got popped. Bolan was an equal-opportunity fucker and reportedly also had sex with his manager Simon Napier-Bell, just hours after the two met. "That is what people did in the '60s," he said. "It wasn't an affair—just a good '60s shag." (*NME*, Aug. 31, 2007)

6. Usher

Usher told a reporter for *Vibe*, "I started having sex at thirteen. I didn't understand why I was having sex until I was about seventeen or eighteen. Let's just say this—I didn't realize that you start to finish. Up until that point, I had never finished. I just always had sex. I understood that I gotta make sure I please this woman, and I hope that her making those noises aren't pain!" (*Vibe*, Oct. 2010)

7. Fergie, Black Eyed Peas

Fergie hung onto her hymen until she was eighteen, but she was rarin' to go from a very young age. "I've always been a very sexual person," confesses the bisexual singer, who once peed her pants onstage. "I've always had to hold myself back—I lost my virginity at eighteen. But that took a lot of willpower." (*Us*, Oct. 15, 2009)

8. Chris Martin (Coldplay)

Does it really surprise anyone that milquetoast Mr. Paltrow kept his pecker in his pants until he was in his twenties? According to the *Guardian*, "Martin, a virgin until the age of twenty-two, with only a handful of girlfriends since, has described himself as 'a failure in all things romantic,' percolating his entire musical oeuvre out of his personal insecurities, as well as death, regret, despair, and other toe-tappers." (*Guardian*, Dec. 7, 2003)

9. Madonna
"I always thought of losing my virginity as a career move." (*Madonna Unauthorized*, 1991)

HONORABLE MENTION

Duane "The Rock" Johnson
Okay, so maybe he's not a rock star, but wrestler-turned-actor Duane Johnson *is* known as the Rock, which is good enough for us. He told *Maxim* magazine, "I was fourteen, she was eighteen, and the cops rolled up on us. Boom, big flashlight on us. They thought bad things were happening when, in actuality, very good things were happening." (*Maxim*, Aug. 2010)

16 VIDEOS THAT WERE TOO HOT FOR TV

Ever since Elvis shook his butt in black and white over the airwaves, TV's been banning scandalous acts. Some get the ax over violence or druggy imagery, but most of the verboten feature nudity and sexual content. Here lies a brief history of the music videos banned for being too boobariffic for the boob tube.

1. "Hurricane," 30 Seconds to Mars
Banned for "overt sexual imagery," Jordan Catalano's vanity project should've been kicked off the airwaves for being that most lethal combination of boring and pretentious.

2. "Smack My Bitch Up," the Prodigy
Drugs, nudity, drunkenness, vomiting, sex, and violence. The perfect storm of mayhem and a good song to boot.

3. "Girls, Girls, Girls," Mötley Crüe
This one should've been subtitled "Nude, Nude, Nude." The band released a tamer, cleaned-up version for airplay, but what good is a song about strippers without nudity?

4. "Girls on Film" (the original version), Duran Duran
The uncensored version of this '80s classic featured scantily clad women doing all manner of things—pillow-fighting while straddling a shaving-cream-covered candy cane; wrestling in the mud, pretending to drown in a kiddie pool, only to be revived by a handsome "lifeguard"; and even sumo wrestling.

5. "Ride," Ciara (featuring Ludacris)
If this video is to be believed, that Ciara knows how to fuck a floor. Shaking that ass in ways that are probably illegal in parts of the south and impossible for most women over twenty, the singer delivers one naughty, albeit ridiculous, video. The highlight is her wet-T-shirt ride on a mechanical bull.

6., 7., and 8. "Peace in the Valley," "Hound Dog," "Heartbreak Hotel," Elvis Presley
Long before there was MTV, there was Ed Sullivan. And Ed's censors were not standing for any shenanigans from the man who'd been dubbed "Elvis the Pelvis" following his first few TV appearances. Presley was scheduled for three performances on Sullivan's show and by the third show the censors had had enough—they didn't censor him, but they shot our boy only from the waist up, sparing the virtue of untold thousands of randy teenage girls.

9. and 10. "Justify My Love," "Erotic," Madonna
That naughty MaTuna—always pushing the buttons. Both were banned for partial nudity, S&M play, and I guess all-around filth. The real issue for most of us was the hilarious gold tooth she wore in the "Justify" video.

11. "Cocoon," Björk
Björk clad in a white body stocking while red licorice strips shoot out of her nips is probably not most people's definition of sexy. Yet this 2001 video by Iceland's number one export was banned because Americans must be shielded from nipples at all costs.

12. "Body Language," Queen
Set in a dimly lit bathhouse, featuring steamed-up models, spankings, nudity, S&M, and homoerotic undertones, this video had the honor of being the first video banned from MTV for all the aforementioned qualities. The song's terribleness apparently didn't play any part in its banning.

13. "Prison Sex," Tool

That the video for a song called "Prison Sex" didn't make MTV's rotation isn't exactly a surprise. But it's too bad because the crazy, scary puppetry in the video makes it one of the more original videos out there. Also, sadly, no actual prison sex.

14. "Closer," Nine Inch Nails

There's no fucking "you like an animal" in the version that was finally neutered enough for MTV's standards. Nor were there any of the crucified monkeys, full-frontal (female) nudity, blindfolded Trent hanging from the ceiling, ball gags, vulva illustrations, or microphones being fellated, that made this video a classic. Though it was too racy for MTV in its original form, New York's well-known purveyors of filth, the Museum of Modern Art, made it part of their permanent collection.

15. "Bück Dich," Rammstein

Where to begin…the simulated sodomy with the ball-gagged band member? Or the dildo spewing gallons of "semen" out over the crowd? Rammstein is a rare breed and also one of the few real competitors Gwar has in the grossness category.

16. "Me So Horny," 2 Live Crew

Back in 1990, 2 Live Crew blew up after a Florida judge banned sales of *Nasty as They Wanna Be* because several of the album's lyrics were said to have "violated community standards for obscenity." Band members were arrested, the owner of a record store was busted after he refused to stop selling the record, and MTV flat-out refused to play the song. A cleaned-up version of the video eventually ran, but it was missing pivotal lines like "Put your lips on my dick and suck my asshole too." Oh, MTV…

NO JUDGMENTS HERE:
15 BANDS NAMED AFTER KINKY
AND BIZARRE SEX PRACTICES

1. Alien Sex Fiend
2. Bondage A Go Go
3. Candy Striper Death Orgy
4. Genitorturers
5. Hentai Cum Dungeon
6. Incubus
7. Kamikazi Sex Pilots
8. Lubricated Goat
9. Midget Handjob
10. Nunfuckers
11. Sex Slaves
12. Sex Gang Children
13. Toilet Böys
14. Tupelo Chain Sex
15. The Velvet Underground

JOE MCGINTY'S 11 SEXY MOMENTS IN THE HISTORY OF ROCK (AND NONROCK) KEYBOARDS

1. Late 1800s
Scott Joplin, while playing gigs in bordellos (to drown out the sexy moans of the patrons), starts to improvise, invents ragtime and jazz.

2. 1950s
Esquerita dons wigs and makeup, becomes rock 'n' roll's first "drag" performer—big influence on Little Richard.

3. 1950s
Jerry Lee Lewis sits on, stands on, and otherwise abuses his piano (and spouses).

4. 1960s
Liberace commissions a rhinestone-encrusted piano and matching suit; inspires Elton John.

5. 1960s
Schroeder's mastery of the toy piano causes Lucy to have an everlasting, unrequited crush on him.

6. Late 1960s
The harpsichord becomes the sexy instrument of choice, as played by Lurch, Laurie Partridge, and the Left Banke.

7. 1970s
Stevie Wonder. 'Nuff said.

8. 1970s
Keith Emerson uses Moog synthesizer controller as a phallic symbol.

9. 1975
Roger Daltrey plays Franz Liszt—and a harpsichord—in Ken Russell's *Lisztomania*.

10. 1970s

Shag carpets, water beds, black lights, and Barry White's crooning (and freewheelin' piano glisses) set the mood for many a smooth seduction.

11. 1982

Wendy and Lisa in Prince's "1999" video. Hottt!

Joe McGinty is an NYC-based keyboardist who was a member of the Psychedelic Furs. He's also worked with the Ramones, Deborah Harry, Ryan Adams, Nada Surf, Ronnie Spector, Mary Weiss, Space Hog, and many others. He runs a vintage keyboard studio in Brooklyn. More info at JoeMcGinty.com.

19 SLIGHTLY UNUSUAL SEXUAL PROCLIVITIES AND PECCADILLOES AND THE SONGS THAT PAY TRIBUTE TO THEM

1. Threesomes

The Byrds' "Triad" is all about the pleasures of the threesome. Which is all well and good, except David Crosby wrote this song. Now think about Crosby being the jiggling blob of man meat in a flesh sandwich and you'll understand why the other Byrds weren't so keen to release it.

2. Foursomes

Happy Mondays' Shaun Ryder was always so messed up, it's doubtful he could get it up with one other person in the room, let alone four. But "Bob's Yer Uncle" describes a scene where "four fall in a bed, three giving head, one getting wet." Notice they do not detail what that wet spot might consist of.

3. Chubby-chasing

AC/DC's Bon Scott was so impressed by the sexual prowess of an obese woman he bedded in Australia that he wrote the song "Whole Lotta Rosie" about the experience. Because it's one of the band's most popular songs, for a while, they even toured with a giant blowup of the mythical chunkette. Things got a little more specific with Queen's "Fat Bottomed Girls" and Sir Mix-a-Lot's "Baby Got Back."

4. The kind of sex you have after you've been up all night freebasing

Okay, so the lyrics to "Super Freak" don't actually allude to such practices, but you know that's what Rick James was talking about, bitch.

5. Phone sex

Remember chat lines? No? Well, then you probably don't remember a time before e-mail either. Anyway, back when dinosaurs roamed the earth and people weren't tweeting their latest bowel movement, long-distance lovers had to rely on phone sex for satisfaction. Reggae singer J. C. Lodge wrote and performed an ode to it, called "Telephone Love." So did the Village People ("Sex over the Phone"), Trina ("Phone Sexx"), and Superchunk ("Phone Sex").

6. Premature ejaculation

While it's more of a problem than a proclivity, Missy Elliott realized the plight of the Preemie Wieners and wrote a sensitive song about the issue, called "One Minute Man." Sing along now: "Ooooooh…I don't want I don't need I can't stand no minute man." Singer/songwriter Jason Mraz sticks up for the Quick-Draw McGraws of the world in his song "Clockwatchers," crooning, "Well so what if a two-pump chump can't last." Well, as long as you don't plan on trying to stick it to Missy, you'll be fine.

7. Analgesic sex

The power of the orgasm is a wondrous thing. It can lift your mood, relieve tension—even calm your cravings for junk food. Marvin Gaye knew all this and more as evidenced by his hit "Sexual Healing," and the wise Peaches is carrying his torch with her admonishment that we "Fuck the Pain Away."

8. Hyperpossessiveness

Stalking's gotten such a bad rap lately, hasn't it? And it's so easy these days, what with Facebook, Foursquare, and a million other ways to track your beliked's every move. Sting has said he's disturbed that the Police's creepy "Every Breath You Take" is used in so many weddings. Blondie's "One Way or Another" offers a less sinister look at the phenom, while Shirley Manson and Garbage get a little more bunny-boiler in "#1 Crush." But stalking isn't all scary as evidenced by the saddest (and prettiest) stalker song, Mazzy Star's "Give You My Lovin'."

9. Autoerotic asphyxiation

Though INXS's Michael Hutchence will forever be known as the poster boy for this particular perversion, Barenaked Ladies did a poppy tune called "I'll Be That Girl," about a young lady who ties a pair of pantyhose around her neck, wanks it, and then ends up dead. Kids, please don't try this one at home.

10. Objectum sexuality

Did you hear the one about the woman who married the Eiffel Tower? Or the lady who pledged her love to the Berlin Wall? Or the nut who whispers sweet nothings to a carnival ride? These are all real people who are truly in love with inanimate objects. Not surprisingly, this love that can't speak its name (because, uh, it doesn't have a mouth) has had a few songs written about it. Bow Wow Wow's "Sexy Eiffel Tower" is a joyous tribute to the French phallic building, while "The Test of Love and Sex" by Fun with Animals is all about having it off with robots.

11. Nocturnal emissions

Bobby Darin's "Dream Lover" might not have been about waking up to sticky sheets, but late Pink Floyd founder Richard Wright's solo album *Wet Dream* wasn't fooling anyone with the pool on the cover, nor is the rap group of the same name or Pretty Ricky's song titled—what else—"Wet Dreams."

12. Symphorophilia

J. G. Ballard's *Crash* is about people who became so aroused by car crashes that they stage their own. (Yes, that's what symphorophilia is.) Years before David Cronenberg adapted it into a movie, a little-known new wave band called the Normal did a song inspired by it, called "Warm Leatherette." "Hear the crushing steel / Feel the steering wheel," went the words; the song was later covered by Grace Jones and Duran Duran.

13. BDSM

From the Crystals' "He Hit Me (It Felt like a Kiss)" to the Velvet Underground's "Venus in Furs" to the Stooges' "I Wanna Be Your Dog" to X-Ray Spex's "Oh Bondage, Up Yours!," there's no shortage of songs about the ouchier side of sex. The Rolling Stones want you under their collective thumb, while icky Nickelback explain that they've "Figured You Out." But BDSM really hit the mainstream when teen heartthrob Justin Timberlake revealed his sub side in "Sexy Back," crooning, "I'm your slave. I'll let you whip me when I misbehave."

14. Urolagnia
If you can name a perversion, chances are the Mentors have a song about it. (And if they don't, GG Allin and the Murder Junkies do.) So yes, getting the "extra 'e' for extra pee" is covered in their song "Golden Showers." Ray J would be so proud.

15. Gender identity fluidity
What would you do if you woke up and found yourself a different sex? Whereas most men might spend the day playing with their new boobies in the mirror, Robyn Hitchcock would immediately get him/herself off in the shower, as evidenced by the lyrics of "Sometimes I Wish I Was a Pretty Girl." The UK indie rock band James wrote about life as a lady in their song "Laid," singing "Dressed me up in women's clothes and messed around with gender roles."

16. Exhibitionism
Paul McCartney was apparently inspired by watching a pair of rutting monkeys when he wrote "Why Don't We Do It in the Road," but public sex is one of the most common fantasies around. Aerosmith's "Love in an Elevator," naughty Trina's "Sex in Public," John Legend's "PDA," and P. J. Harvey's "Sheela-Na-Gig" (P. J. also gets extra points for the "dirty pillows"/*Carrie* reference) are but a few others.

17. Spanking
The *thwack* of hand against ass is the lighter side of the BDSM spectrum and has been the subject of many songs. Akon propositioned his lady by asking her back to his place where he would "possibly bend you over, look back and watch me smack that" in his hit "Smack That." Madonna was begging for it in "Hanky Panky," and Chris Isaak was making promises in "Baby Did a Bad, Bad Thing." It's not all men doing the spanking, though, as Chrissie Hynde growled in the Pretenders song "Bad Boys Get Spanked."

18. Necrophilia
While sex with dead people certainly isn't many people's cup of tea, there are plenty of songs about it—and they're not all Norwegian black metal. TSOL's "Code Blue" is one of the catchier numbers, but other bands who've gone there include GG Allin (shocking, eh?) with "I Fuck the Dead," the Misfits with "Last Caress," the Hoodoo Gurus with "Dig It Up," and the ultracreepy Comus with "Drip Drip."

19. Fisting

Also known as "handballing," fisting involves inserting the hand into the anus or vagina. There are many fisting fans; therefore there are many songs about it, including Tricky's "I Like the Girl," Nine Inch Nails' "Fist Fuck," and the always festive "Fist Me This Christmas," by the Wet Spots. Of Montreal released a song with the misleading title "Teenage Unicorn Fisting," but, sadly, it wasn't about unicorns or fisting at all. Just an indie rock joke.

8 BANDS NAMED AFTER PROCREATION GONE WRONG

1. Comanche Abortion
2. Dance Me Pregnant
3. Dayglo Abortions
4. Deep-Fried Abortions
5. Gay Witch Abortion
6. Peter and the Test Tube Babies
7. Rhythm Method
8. Scraping Foetus from the Wheel (and all the other Foetus incarnations)

8 OOZING, BURNING, PUS–ENCRUSTED, STD–MONIKERED BANDS

1. Burning Fallus
2. Discharge
3. Electric Gonorrhea
4. Gonorrhea Pussy
5. Herpes
6. Pissing Razors
7. Specimen
8. Syphilitic Vaginas

NOT GETTING ANY

ATTACK OF THE VAGINA-DRYERS!
12 CONCERT EXPERIENCES THAT WILL
ENSURE YOU WON'T GET LAID

Rock shows are traditionally a great venue for a quick pickup. There's the beat, the booze, the broads and boys, all sweaty and ready to go. Rock is primal, like sex. So as you're shakin' that ass, it's natural that you start thinking about whom you'd like to shake it with. Yet there are some bands that are the aural equivalent of a big bucket of cold water. Hearing them is like stumbling upon a copy of your parents' sex tape or accidentally downing a bowl of saltpeter.

In the interest of being servicey, here are twelve bands to avoid if you want to get laid.

1. Rush

It's a little-known fact that Rush's guitars are tuned to a secret frequency that causes the normally moist, elastic walls of the vagina to dry, contract, and seal themselves shut. Their appeal to the ladies is not helped by the fact that Geddy Lee is the fugliest man in rock, bar none.

2. Yes

No.

3. Justin Bieber

Though the hordes of shrieking tweens are all moist and nubile, go there and you're looking at a felony conviction. You might get lucky if you're into MILFs, but after an hour of Bieber squeaking, your balls will retreat into your body and you'll be rendered impotent anyway.

4. ELP

While it's true that the trio of Keith Emerson, Greg Lake, and Carl Palmer were actually pretty cute back in the day, these prog-rock superstars' oeuvre is the erotic equivalent of a warm turd. You might want to solve physics problems or alphabetize your cast of Dungeons and Dragons characters while listening, but you won't even want to have sex with yourself once you hear "Still You Turn Me On."

5. Jonas Brothers

Like Bieber, the Jo Bros attract a young, overwhelmingly female crowd, but unlike the Biebs, they also have a Christian element, which means even their fans' moms are off-limits.

6. Edgar and/or Johnny Winter

While these albino bluesmen are very talented, their lack of pigmentation can be a turn-off to the fairer sex. The main reason you're more likely to get laid after a rock show is because the band has lubed up all the ladies and spared you the need for foreplay. When the band is fug, you need to work twice as hard.

7. Any straight-edge band

Ian MacKaye from Minor Threat once barked, "Don't smoke, don't drink, don't fuck." The lyrics left unsaid: "Don't have any fun either." Sure, there's always a possibility you'll be able to pick up some sassy little thing with an "X" Sharpied across the back of her hand, but there's also a chance you'll wind up getting a lecture on Hare Krishna or veganism instead of the blowie you were hoping for.

8. Owl City

Minnesota's Adam Young is an attractive, talented young guy who records under the name of Owl City. What gives Owl City such a neutering influence is that Young is afflicted with that sunken-chested wimpiness so epidemic in indie-rockers these days. More herbal tea than Jack-and-coke, Owl City is pure milquetoast. The band's merch even includes an infantilizing (but grown-up-sized) *onesie*. Kids today.

9. Hawkwind

The band that spawned—and then spat out—Motörhead's Lemmy, attracts a crowd that's equal parts biker, sci-fi dork, and metal dude. Guesstimates place the audience makeup at about 99.9 percent male. The tiny fraction of females in the crowd have inevitably been dragged there by their hairier halves. The band's take on space rock is the anti-aphrodisiac, which explains the dearth of any sort of sexual energy in any venue they blast with their presence.

10. GG Allin and the Murder Junkies

Though you might have convinced some drunk broad to blow you after a GG Allin show, there'd also have been a good chance you'd have to flick GG fluids or excrement out of her hair first. Then again, if you knowingly attended a GG Allin show, and then were able to get it up afterwards, you pretty much got what you deserved. Rest in peace, GG.

11. Venom, Emperor, Mayhem, and most other black metal bands

Burning churches, Nazi imagery, and the occasional murder are bad enough, but the cartoonishly ridiculous growled or shrieked vocals about bloodletting and Satan ensure that the majority of fans of this genre are disaffected teenage boys slathered in Proactiv and wearing pentagram-emblazoned denim vests. In short: Though the flames of hell may be scorching, these bands are definitely *not* hot.

12. Free jazz

There's always a price to pay when you're talking free jazz and, unfortunately, that cost is usually exacted on your libido. Noodling solos, discordant crescendos, and self-indulgent screeching improvisations are the hallmarks of this genital-deadening genre.

ZACHARY LIPEZ'S 11 VERY GOOD REASONS NOT TO HAVE SEX IN THAT FILTHY ROCK BAR BATHROOM

11. She never pays for drinks at any bar owned by Jesse Malin and Johnny T and avoids eye contact when you ask her why.

10. Who cares if he's Iggy Pop and it's 1972—you're fifteen years old and it's not too late to decide to become a phlebotomist or an architect, rather than a footnote in someone else's stupid history.

9. If she dresses like Stevie Nicks and will let anything besides cocaine be put up her butt, she's a fucking poseur.

8. He has an ironic tattoo in an area where irony should play no part.

7. You put on "This Corrosion" by Sisters of Mercy. That gives you 10:55 to do whatever you think is best: 1:00 to navigate your way to the bathroom; 1:30 to explain to the fifteen girls in line why you have to cut in front of them and why, just because you're a girl and the DJ, they don't actually *have* to be shitty and passive-aggressive about it (phrase it as a request, maintain the moral high ground, threaten to affect their ability to obtain drinks); another 30 seconds to explain to the weirdo last in line that they're welcome to join you. The pounding on the door will start immediately. If it's not security (and it never is), ignore it. 7:55. Introduce yourself. She's sweet but doing that weird, lip-biting thing that you got sick of in 2003. Now you have five minutes, and you're wearing incredibly complicated stockings under shorts under longish shirt combo. And the belt? Don't even get me started on the belt. You're also not really a lesbian. Just do the drugs.

6. With the invention of the Internet you no longer have to have your butt thrust into a sink for six awkward minutes while the strains of "Hold on Tight (to Your Dreams)" filter under the door as some slumming Wesleyan grad student's multiple beaded necklaces get tangled in your bangs, to completely annihilate your sense of self-worth. Join Match.com; keep your heinie dry.

5. Yeah, sure, a greater power, okay, some sort of vague source wherein all life and energy is derived; maybe but, maybe, and just maybe, something to think about while you're using Arcade Fire to maintain some sort of grandeur in the most squalid situations, maybe there's an actual being, an omnipotent being, who, yes, sure, is capable of an all-encompassing love, an omnipotent love, that's possible but, and I don't need to tell you this, there's the flip side to the omnipotent love, an omnipotent being capable of, I'm not trying to be a downer but you're no stranger to what is commonly referred to as a "moment of clarity" and therefore know this can be true too, an omnipotent contempt. What you're doing isn't kind. And just because the Paul Simons of the world have abandoned conventional notions of right and wrong for the easy allure of wholesale cultural theft and lazy Hollywood liberalism, that doesn't mean that we no longer get to

care about our immortal souls. Remove your underwear from the hand dryer. There you go. Now go reward yourself with a nice gin gimlet.

4. If joining Narcotics Anonymous makes you a Jet, and joining Alcoholics Anonymous makes you a Shark, then this love is forbidden and can only lead to heartbreak and open-dance warfare. And not one person in this club can actually dance.

3. None of the Strokes hang out in bars anymore. Regardless what he says, that dude is totally not in the Strokes.

2. You're going to let someone whose idea of a cognizant argument is "Well, their FIRST record wasn't racist" put their PENIS INSIDE of you?

1. She doesn't love you, dude. Not really.

Zachary Lipez is the leader singer for Freshkills and, with Stacey Wakefield and Nick Zinner, coauthor of the books *No Seats on the Party Car, Slept in Beds,* and *Please Take Me Off the Guest List.* He's been working the bars of New York City for over a decade.

5 BANDS WHO PRACTICE EXTREME SELF-LOVE

1. Accu Jack and the Self Abusers
2. Circle Jerks
3. Danger Wank
4. Meat Beat Manifesto
5. The Strokes

17 SONGS ABOUT JERKIN' OFF

You'd think that since John Mayer makes the O-face every time he picks up the guitar, he'd have a song about yankin' it, but you'd be mistaken. These seventeen are not so shy.

I. "Icicle," Tori Amos
Naughty bit: "Getting off, getting off while they're all downstairs."

2. "Rock My World," Betty Blowtorch
Naughty bit: "My panties are wet, once again you're too damn late / Sorry there baby, I had to masturbate."

3. "St. Swithin's Day," Billy Bragg
Naughty bit: "When I make love to your memory, it's not the same."

4. "Girls of Porn," Mr. Bungle
Naughty bit: "My hand gets tired and my dick gets sore / But the girls of porn want more."

5. "Orgasm Addict," Buzzcocks
Naughty bit: "Sneakin' in the back door with dirty magazines / And your mother wants to know what are those stains on your jeans."

6. "Praying Hands," Devo
Naughty bit: This song describes something reminiscent of "the stranger," wherein you lie on top of one arm until the blood stops flowing and then you use that hand to beat off with so it feels like a stranger is touching you.

7. "I Touch Myself," the Divinyls
Naughty bit: "When I think about you I touch myself."

8. "Dancing with Myself," Billy Idol
Naughty bit: The "dancing" Billy's referring to is obviously a euphemism for the five-knuckle shuffle.

9. "She Bop" Cyndi Lauper
Naughty bit: "They say I better stop or I'll go blind."

I0. "Darling Nikki," Prince
Naughty bit: "I met her in a hotel lobby / Masturbating with a magazine."

II. "Homemade," Sebadoh
Naughty bit: "Sittin' around with my homemade bone."

12. "All By Myself," Johnny Thunders and the Heartbreakers

Naughty bit: "What's that dripping in your hand?"

13. "Oops (Oh My)," Tweet

Naughty bit: "Umm, and I was feelin' so good I had to touch myself."

14. "Turning Japanese," the Vapors

Naughty bit: "I'm turning Japanese" allegedly (and politically incorrectly) refers to the way your eyes squint as you get yourself off.

15. "Blister in the Sun," Violent Femmes

Naughty bit: Note to Violent Femmes: If you're yanking it so often you develop blisters, you need to give it a rest for a few days.

16. "Mr. Richard Smoker," Ween

Naughty bit: "You're a chicken choker."

17. "Pictures of Lily," the Who

Naughty bit: When Junior can't sleep, his dad gives him naughty photographs and indeed, "Pictures of Lily helped me feel alright [*sic*]."

MINOR THREAT GUITARIST STEVE HANSGEN'S 13 DOWNSIDES TO BEING STRAIGHT EDGE

"(I) don't smoke (I) don't drink (I) don't fuck! At least I can fucking think...."

—Ian MacKaye, "Out of Step," 1981

I would like to start this "list" by simply stating that what I am about to write is largely (but not entirely) tongue-in-cheek and at the same time totally serious.

As a greater metropolitan DC–area punk rock teenager in the early 1980s, I was a true believer in what was then *not* known as the straight edge. "Straight Edge" was a song by Minor Threat, not a movement. The fact that many of us teen punks didn't drink, use drugs, or smoke was fairly coincidental and an outsider's badge of pride.

But, like many legitimately good ideas, it had its drawbacks. Especially for painfully shy and socially inept teenage boys . . .

1. Complete, total and utter SEXUAL FRUSTRATION due to the (I) Don't Fuck "clause" and the peer pressure put on one to comply to it.

2. Social ineptitude (as if most of us needed any help in that department) brought on by a feeling of superiority because you are "straight" and everyone else is "not."

3. A false, but deeply held, feeling of superiority (see above), which pissed everyone off. Especially girls. *Especially* cute girls.

4. Coming across as being—and in fact actually being—incredibly uptight.

5. Complete, total, and utter SEXUAL FRUSTRATION.

6. Outside of truly great punk rock shows, having a pretty boring, and at times depressing, social life.

7. Hanging out with people who are as sexually frustrated (mostly), boring, pedantic, socially inept, and arrogant as yourself. PARTY!!!!

8. Parties where the only interesting thing that happens is Guy Picciotto (original DC punk and later a member of the hugely influential DC punk bands Rites of Spring and Fugazi) gets naked and sits in a tub of ice cream in order to make "butt prints." It sounds like more fun that it actually was....

9. Complete, total, and utter SEXUAL FRUSTRATION.

10. Being harassed all across this great country of ours by other punk rockers for being "prissy Goody Two-shoes" or "preachy monks." Especially in Los Angeles and San Francisco (I love both cities as a real live growned-up person though, btw).

11. As a member of pioneering straight-edge band Minor Threat, being asked to explain the straight edge to quite literally EVERY SINGLE PERSON WHO INTERVIEWED US. The concept seemed pretty straightforward at the time, which is why we got pretty testy about constantly having to explain or defend it. I sincerely apologize now if I was ever rude to you.

12. Complete, total, and utter SEXUAL FRUSTRATION.

13. Watching this basically great idea become a distorted version of itself by (largely) well-meaning punks in cities all across America and abroad. We never meant for anyone to get beat up because they were drinking, smoking, doing drugs or…fucking at a punk show. Honestly. And if you were, I apologize, sincerely.

I'm sure I could come up with more downsides but the sour-grapes quotient is getting pretty full and by now I am sure you get the idea! It wasn't all bad, but when it was, it truly sucked! And when it was good, it was as good as anything ever was.

Steve Hansgen is the former bass player with DC punk bands Minor Threat and Government Issue and the current bass player of DC geezer-punk band Rustbuckit. He is married (yes, he finally got over himself!) to an amazing woman named Nuit, and they have a beautiful son named Jack. They reside in the bucolic wilds of Howard County, Maryland. Steve is still friends with many of his fellow DC punk rockers.

5 ROCKERS WHO (ALLEGEDLY) KEEP IT IN THEIR PANTS (AND ONE WHO DIDN'T)

Along with the guitars, the tats, the drinking and drugging, rock stars are known for being great big ho-bags. Sluttiness is practically part of their job requirement—right up there with leather pants and guitar picks. Sure, you get the occasional aberration like the Jonas Brothers and their purity rings, but more common are the penis-driven Bret Michaels and Angus Youngs of the world. Speaking of Angus, it was he who once opined, "My fantasy [guitar] would be a cannon that shot sperm at the audience." (Sorry, Angus. Gwar already beat you to that.)

Here are five (yeah, I could only find five) rockers who prove that there are some things that are more important than meaningless sex with faceless groupies…or at least five smart enough to say the right thing to the reporter so they don't get their ass kicked at home.

I. Mike Monroe

"[O]ne doesn't have to be a sleazeball to be a rock 'n' roller and I don't like to be conceived as one. You see, I'm happily married with one woman and I never cheat. Even in my years alone, I was never into groupies." (Interview with Saviours of Rock)

2. Eddie Vedder

"Pearl Jam lead singer Eddie Vedder was one of a few rock stars with a reputation of being faithful to his wife. But now he's divorced (his wife reportedly cheated on him), and one of the first women Eddie dated after the breakup was a model. In other words, Eddie's turned into a typical rock star." (Groupiedirt.com)

3. Russell Brand

"My wife recently explained to me, 'You must be faithful' and I don't have a problem with that. I'm really, really in love.... You just can't maraud through life fucking whoever you'd like—which is a shame, because I wish I actually could do that. That's the compromise." (Interview with the *Sun*—he counts because he's married to a pop star.)

4. Bono

"I have a great mate. You know, I have a great friend in Ali. And you know, I like being in her company, and...you exercise restraint. That's what you do. And you know, that's it, but I mean, I'm just—I'm in love." (Interview with Larry King, Dec. 1, 2001, though there are rumors about his fidelity . . .)

5. Charlie Watts (who's been married for nearly forty years)

"Girls chasing you down the street, screaming...horrible! I hated it. It was quite flattering, I suppose. And it's fantastic to play to audiences like that. For me, that was the whole point of being chased down the street.... Playing the drums was all I was ever interested in. The rest of it made me cringe." (*Guardian*, July 9, 2000)

(DIS)HONORABLE MENTION

Turns out that Britney Spears was NOT that innocent!

Britney Spears claimed she was a virgin well into her twenties, but according to at least one person who used to be on her payroll, Brit lost her virginity much earlier. According to ex-lawyer Eric Ervin, Brit and Justin Timberlake were getting *dirrrrty* from jump. (*Daily Mail*, Nov. 21, 2007)

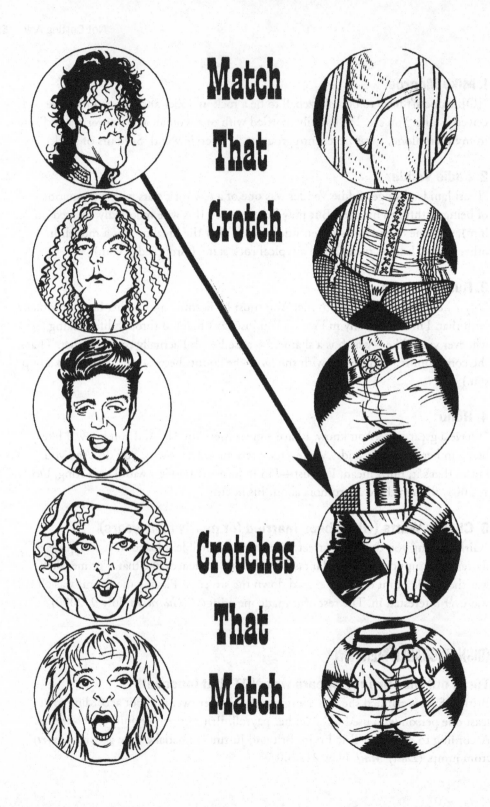

NAUGHTY BITS

3

ERIN BRADLEY'S 10 MOST ICONIC CROTCHES IN ROCK HISTORY

Elvis Presley could carry a tune, but it was his pelvis that made him famous. Looking for the heart of rock 'n' roll? Start in the groin region. Whether pouring their hips into leather pants or gyrating their scantily clad torsos in bondage gear, rock legends have long made a focal point of their nether regions.

1. David Lee Roth
If your average crotch is a sensible gray sedan, Roth's is a tricked-out yellow Ferrari. Never has a male member been so accessorized…or so athletic. Whether posing for pinup mags in assless chaps or jumping spread-eagle off trampolines, Roth boasts a lower body that's 50 percent West Texas pageant girl, 50 percent coked-up peacock. The result? One hundred percent pure magnificence.

2. Madonna
Most of us grew up with Madonna's crotch. It's as American as McDonald's apple pie or tech support from India. We've seen it all—in everything from leotards to peekaboo skirts to gold lamé Gaultier onesies. Is it time for Madge to give it a rest?

Why don't you spend that much time getting in shape and then see if you're not tempted to flaunt your nethers up and down every available street?

3. Elvis

It's the crotch that launched a million fans and an equal number of tacky collector plates. Elvis swiveled his lower half with such aplomb that Florida lawmakers threatened to arrest him for indecency. Note that he performed fully clothed, singing lyrics like, "I wanna be your teddy bear." Racy!

4. Prince

Whether he's strutting around in bikini underwear or using his guitar as a makeshift phallic prop in front of a Super Bowl audience of millions, this pocket-size sex symbol has never had a problem when it comes to below-the-belt self-esteem. His crotch looks better in lingerie than most women's.

5. Robert Plant

Loopy songs about hobbits aside, Plant's contribution to the jean-boner genre ranks among rock's most notable achievements. Witness the taut interplay of denim and flesh, the bold belt, the undone shirt casually thrown about the shoulders, all of it carefully choreographed to draw attention to that one vital organ: "What, this old thing?"

6. Lady Gaga

Poor Lady Gaga and her gaga. Not since Rod Stewart's bellyful of protein shake have asinine rumors run this wild and free. What's going on under there? Is she male? Female? Some type of mystery meat? Here's hoping the rumors continue their slow fade so we can get back to the business of loving or hating her music, respectively.

7. Axl Rose

Dear Axl's Crotch,
It seems like only yesterday that you caught our eye in the "Welcome to the Jungle" video. Hypnotic, you were. Like a cobra in a pair of leather pants. And even though cobras can't really wear pants, we think you know what we mean. White-bicycle-shorts phase be damned—a lower torso like that means never having to say you're sorry.

8. Courtney Love

Long before celebrity upskirts came into vogue, Love was doing her own take. With torn-up granny panties, bruised upper thighs, and freewheelin' pubic hair, the look was anything but mainstream-ready. Nice girls are taught to "keep their legs closed" and "sit like a lady." Courtney's crotch seems to say, "Fuck off, I'm a rock star, and you can't make me."

9. Steven Tyler

Music fashions come and go. (Remember when Dr. Dre looked like an extra on *Star Trek*?) Tyler's dick-hugger jumpsuits, many of them handmade by his ex-wife, have been his pelvic trademark since the early '70s. You could argue that, at sixty-two, Tyler is getting a little old to be showing off his package. Maybe so, but some dangly bits deserve our respect. You don't throw a cover over the *Mona Lisa*.

10. Michael Jackson

Yeah, we know. But to not write about the man who made the crotch-grab a de rigueur dance move feels strangely revisionist. All we're saying is, everyone from five to fifty can do at least part of the "Thriller" dance some thirty years after the album's release. Not since the invention of the bikini wax has someone so altered the course of pop-culture crotch history.

This article originally appeared on Nerve.com in July 2010. Erin Bradley is the author of *Every Rose Has Its Thorn: The Rock 'n' Roll Field Guide to Guys*, available at RockOutWithYourBookOut.com. She also spent five years writing Miss Information, a sex and dating advice column on Nerve.com.

5 OF THE BIGGEST UNITS IN ROCK

1. Nick Cave

Tall, skinny guys are often blessed with larger-than-life packages. Mr. Cave confirmed this rumor, telling one reporter, "Well, I was gonna pull my dick out but because I know for a fact mine is a lot larger than Jim Morrison's, I thought, 'I'll let history stand.'" (Spinner.com, Oct. 23, 2008)

2. Jay-Z

According to a groupie message board, Mr. Beyoncé is rockin' "the biggest dick you will ever see in your life…like a one-liter Pepsi bottle…It's beyond huge. It could block the sun." (OzoneMagazine.com)

3. Tommy Lee

His member is so massive it demanded its own font in his memoir, *Tommyland*. If you saw the infamous Pam Anderson sex tape, you will know that seeing is believing.

4. Tony Kanal

No wonder Gwen wrote "Don't Speak" about their relationship. Who can talk when you're trying to handle what several groupie message boards assure the world is a ten-incher?

5. Iggy Pop

As one groupie put it, "Iggy's cock is so big it could have its own zip code."

38 BANDS WHO PAID HOMAGE TO THE WEENUS BY NAMING THEMSELVES AFTER THEIR MOST USEFUL APPENDAGE

1. Ballcock Assembly
2. Black Cock
3. The Broken Penis Orchestra
4. Buzzcocks
5. Captain Beefheart
6. Cock and Ball Torture
7. Cocks in Stained Satin
8. Dick Cheese and the Crackers
9. Dick Delicious and the Tasty Testicles
10. The Dick Panthers
11. Dickies
12. Dickless
13. The Dicks

14. 4-Skins
15. Gaggle of Cocks
16. GoatPenis
17. Goblin Cock
18. Hard-Ons
19. Iron Prostate
20. Jefferson's Cock
21. Juzt Nutz
22. Limp Bizkit
23. Little Richard
24. Mega Smegma
25. Monster Cock Rally
26. Penis Flytrap
27. Prick
28. Revolting Cocks
29. Rumpleforeskin
30. Satan's Almighty Penis
31. Scrotum Grinder
32. Scrotum Pole
33. Sex Pistols
34. Smegma and the Nuns
35. Steaming Wolf Penis
36. The Testostertones (an all-male a cappella ensemble)
37. Throbbing Gristle
38. Whitesnake

17 BANDS NAMED IN HOMAGE TO THAT NEGLECTED ORIFICE, THE ASSHOLE

1. Anal Blasphemy
2. Anal Blast
3. Anal Cunt
4. Anal Seepage
5. Ass Ponys
6. Asspounder

7. Assfactor 4
8. Buck Naked and the Bare Bottom Boys
9. Big Ass
10. Butthole Surfers
11. Butt Stomach
12. Butt Trumpet
13. Fudge Tunnel
14. Hot Buttered Anal
15. The Meat Shits
16. Mighty Sphincter
17. The Skids

8 BANDS NAMED AFTER SPOOGE

1. Creaming Jesus
2. Crowned in Semen
3. Pearl Jam
4. Premature Ejaculation
5. SpermSwamp
6. Spunk
7. 10cc
8. Thin White Rope (Burroughs's term for ejaculation)

18 BANDS NAMED IN TRIBUTE TO THE GLORIOUS LADY FLOWER

1. Barney Rubble and the Cunt Stubble
2. Box Squad
3. Clit Boys
4. Cunts
5. Electric Vagina
6. Flaming Lips
7. The F.C.C. (Flying Cunts of Chaos)
8. Hole
9. Nashville Pussy
10. Ovarian Trolley
11. Pabst Smear (Honorable mention to Pat Smear from the Germs)
12. Pussy Finger
13. Pussy Galore
14. Pussy Pirates
15. The Slits
16. Snatch Magnet
17. Vulvathrone
18. Yeastie Girlz

WHO DON'T LIKE BOOBIES? 5 BANDS NAMED FOR TITS!

1. The Fierce Nipples
2. Les Breastfeeders
3. The Nipple Erectors (later known as the Nips)
4. Swingin' Utters
5. T.I.T.S.

WOMEN'S STUDIES

4

THEO KOGAN'S 10 WORST THINGS ABOUT DATING A GIRL IN A BAND: THIS IS A WARNING !!!

1. She's always touring, never home.
2. Her band is more important than you are.
3. She's self-/voice-/guitar-/drum-/bass-obsessed.
4. Creepy guys will follow her while she's out on the road.
5. Creepy girls will follow her while she's out on the road.
6. She might break up with you while she's out on the road.
7. She might be sleeping with as many people as the dudes in bands do while *they're* out on the road.
8. She may "lose" her phone.
9. She may come back from tour totally uninterested in you.
10. That guy who picked up her phone at 3 a.m.? He's actually *not* her drummer, her gay BFF, or her brother.

Theo Kogan is the lead singer of Theo and the Skyscrapers, a DJ, model, actress, and, most recently, a mom. She was a founding member of the notorious Lunachicks and recently started a beauty line called Armour Beauty (ArmourBeauty.com).

BAD RELIGION'S TOUR MANAGER, CATHY MASON, TELLS THE 10 WORST THINGS ABOUT BEING THE ONLY GIRL ON THE TOUR BUS

1. I think the worst thing I have come across is the double standard. When I started touring it was very much a man's world and I was laughed at for wanting to do it. Today there is still a double standard. If women sleep around on tour they get fired or put down; if they yell at someone they are called a bitch.

2. If you are a woman in charge, expect some resistance. Some men still find it very hard to take direction from a woman. I have been ignored, spit on, insulted, fought with, etc. There is always someone who will try to push you around or intimidate you.

3. I haven't found it possible to have a loving relationship with my job. It's pretty rare that you can find a man who is okay with staying home for months at a time while you live with ten dudes on a bus.

4. No matter how good you are at your job or how smart you are, you will always be compared to a man. Usually it is because you took your job from a man.

5. Being viewed as a toy or a plaything. You have to prove yourself as worthy to be taken seriously.

6. European venue showers! Imagine yourself in a shower made out of a plastic coffin with no lock, labeled "Men's Room." Do I need to say more?

7. There is never a moment to yourself. From the time we get to the airport to the time I send everyone home I am surrounded. It's a rare moment when I can sneak away by myself.

8. Women are very good at multitasking, so we tend to take on more than most people would ever do. During one day I have more tasks than anyone else on my crew.

9. Being rejected because women do not trust women. I have heard on several occasions that I am perfect for the job, but someone's wife does not want women on tour. It is a very sad truth about women.

10. No toilet paper!

Cathy Mason started in the music business as a marketing intern for Atrophy Pop management and dabbling in accounting for BYO Records. She's been touring for ten years, starting off as the merch girl for bands such as Manic Hispanic, NOFX, and Silverchair. She created a merchant-processing company making it easier for bands to accept credit cards at shows and eventually moved up to tour management. For the past four years, she's been tour-managing Bad Religion.

SARAH JEZEBEL DEVA'S 8 MISCONCEPTIONS ABOUT WOMEN IN BLACK METAL BANDS

1. We sucked all of the male members off so we could get a position in the band.
I normally just use a phone or e-mail.

2. Women can't headbang.
I've seen many men trying to headbang and they look like they are having an epileptic ant-stamping fit! They are just jealous because I have no split ends.

3. Women shouldn't headbang.
I was told this once by a band member. This is the same guy who told me that I didn't need to hear myself in monitors onstage.

4. We shag on graves, drinking red wine, covered in baby powder, constantly do the devil horns, while screaming "SATAN!!" as we climax.
I have been asked so many variations of this and what's this "climax" word everyone is using???

5. We have loads of groupies.
No, we don't have groupies, we have psycho stalkers. They propose to you online, threaten to kill themselves, and they *still* can't spell ya name right.

6. We are goths.

NO!!!! *Huge* difference, I do not listen to the Cure, swaying by candlelight in my bedroom with no mates.

7. We live in castles, have magic powers, and are demon goddesses.

No, I live in an apartment, struggle every month to pay my bills, and I am a housewife.

8. We have all burnt a church and run through the forest naked.

Me? Run? Ha-ha . . .

Sarah Jezebel Deva is best known for her fourteen years in Cradle of Filth as female vocalist. However, she has also sung on more than thirty-five albums for bands such as Therion, Mortiis, and the Kovenant. She has her own band, Angtoria, as well as a career as a solo artist under her own name. Visit http://www.facebook.com/SarahJezebelDeva

DARYL K'S ROCK STAR 5-PIECE WHAT-TO-WEAR

1. Leather leggings
2. Sexy, ripped cool T-shirt in black or white
3. Kick-ass, high-heeled cowboy boots
4. Tailored, aged leather jacket with lots of pockets so you can go out without a bag
5. Lots of chunky silver jewelry

Daryl K is a Dublin-born/NYC-based fashion designer who opened her first store in 1991. She's done wardrobe for Jim Jarmusch films, dressed rock stars such as Kim Gordon, and won a CFDA Perry Ellis Award in 1996. For more guidance, go to DarylK.com.

MICHAEL MUSTO'S LIST OF 11 FILTHY NEW SONGS FOR BRITNEY SPEARS

Britney Spears has carved a lucrative niche out of singing double-entendre sex songs like "If You Seek Amy" and "Hold It Against Me." Well, I've come up with yet another eleven surefire leering, nudge-nudge sex hits for the pop tart to open her mouth to while her tongue wags. She can send the royalty checks to me care of the Voice.

Here goes:

11. "Be Genital with My Love"
10. "Is That a Rocket in Your Pocket?"
9. "On My Knees at the Noodle Shop"
8. "Dress Me Up in Doggy Style"
7. "Sperm Whale (Beach Yourself on Me)"
6. "Touch My Crescent and Taste My Pie" (Baker's Mix)
5. "Voting for You at the Next Erection"
4. "F**k in the Road" (duet with Cee-Lo Green)
3. "Your Body of Work Is Impressive"
2. "I'm Taking Dick Out for Clams"

And the winner . . .

1. "I'm a (WHORE)-d'Oeuvre"

With the flip side:

"My Abandoned Beaver Pond is an Ideal Habitat for Wetland Species"

Michael Musto is a New York institution. He has been writing the hilarious "La Dolce Musto" column since 1984 and recently began a daily blog, both for the *Village Voice*.

GAY STUDIES

9 EXAMPLES OF GAY FAKERY

Though homophobia is rampant enough to drive many people—famous and civilians—into the closet, there are times when playing gay has its benefits.

1. and 2.   Jimi Hendrix and Iggy Pop both pretended to be gay to avoid military service. (Though the jury's still out on whether or not Iggy was *totally* faking it.)

3. Madonna's stunt lesbionics are as faux as her Hogwarts accent. First she and Sandra Bernhard had a prank affair and then she made out with Britney Spears as a TV stunt. Oh, Madge.

4. and 5.   T.A.T.u.'s manager knew that nothing gets certain (i.e., most) men going like hot, barely legal lesbians in schoolgirl outfits. The twosome also garnered a large lesbian following, but it quickly became obvious that both girls had boyfriends and hated making out with each other.

6. Hannah Montana (aka Miley Cyrus) outraged several really sheltered Brits when she fake-kissed a female dancer during an appearance on *Britain's Got Talent*. The rest of the world was too busy still rolling their eyes from her incestu-sexy *Vanity Fair* photo shoot with daddy Billy Ray to care.

7. Eyelinered Fall Out Boy Pete Wentz has feigned gay plenty of times, once even appearing on a cover of *Out* magazine with the quote: "Yeah, I'm a fag." While it sounds like his intentions might have been good, he mostly comes off as a naïve, publicity-seeking moron. Yawn.

8. When Jill Sobule sang "I Kissed a Girl," it was sweet and she meant it. When the once rabidly Christian Katy Perry sang about the same subject in a song with the same title, she was making a cynical grab for attention, much like the sorority girl who makes out with her sister after her third shot of Jäger.

9. It's become somewhat fashionable for women to talk about sexual experiments with other broads, but most men are still too uptight to talk about it, even if they went there. Not Steven Tyler. In his autobiography, *Does the Noise in My Head Bother You?*, he admits to a little man-on-man action but came out of the experience unimpressed. "Gay sex just doesn't do it for me…. I tried it, but I just didn't dig it."

32 OF THE GAYEST BAND NAMES EVER

While not all of these bands were made up exclusively of gay, um, members (rim shot!), they've chosen names that are out and proud.

1. Bear Party
2. Black Fag (queercore Black Flag cover band)
3. Butch Country
4. The Butchies
5. The Colour Pink Is Gay
6. Deep Dickollective
7. Fruit Punch
8. Fudgepackers
9. Gay Baby
10. Gay Beast
11. The Gay Blades
12. Gay for Johnny Depp

13. Gaye Bykers on Acid (Would occasionally open for themselves in drag, billing themselves as "Lesbian Dopeheads on Mopeds" so they could get paid twice.)
14. Girlyman
15. Homer and the Sexuals
16. Hunx and His Punx
17. Jean Genet
18. Limp Wrist
19. My! Gay! Husband!
20. 1,000 Homo DJs (This Al Jourgensen project is very hetero, but the name probably pissed some people off, so we're keeping it.)
21. Pansy Division
22. The Pink Fairies (Though one of them was named Twink, it's unclear whether any of these prog rockers were actually homosexual.)
23. Pink Stëël
24. Queen
25. The Queers
26. Scissorfight
27. Scissor Sisters
28. Shitting Glitter
29. Sissy Boy Slap Party
30. Tribe 8
31. The Village People (Only three of the guys were openly gay.)
32. Youth of Togay

27 RANDOM GAY ROCKERS

I. Little Richard

It's hard to imagine that someone as flamboyant as Little Richard was ever actually in the closet, but he told John Waters in a 1987 interview for *Playboy*, "I believe I was the founder of gay. I'm the one who started to be so bold tellin' the world! You got to remember my dad put me out of the house because of that." (*Guardian*, Nov. 28, 2010)

2. Freddie Mercury

Brian May has a Ph.D. in physics, yet didn't know his (hullo!) Queen bandmate was gay? In 2008, he told a reporter, "I think there was a slight suspicion, but it never occurred to me that he was gay."

3. Rob Halford

It mustn't have been easy for Judas Priest's Rob Halford to come out of the closet. Though the leather-daddy imagery seems pretty obvious now, heavy metal is known for being a rather meatheadish genre. He told the *San Diego Gay and Lesbian News*, "It's a different world now. Heavy metal now is a completely different world compared to heavy metal in 1980. The gay and lesbian world is very different now as it was in 1980. We have all grown to some extent. There is still a long way to go. There are still a lot of issues that need to be addressed, but I think slowly but surely our lives are getting better."

4. Chuck Panozzo

The now openly gay (and, unfortunately HIV-positive) Panozzo wasn't always so comfortable with his sexuality. In a trailer for his 2007 memoir, the Styx bassist says, "I told my brother when I was twenty that I was gay. I had told my sister—she just thought it was a phase. My brother's remark was, 'Now I know why you acted the way you were'—whatever that meant."

5. Doug Pinnick

The King's X leader reflected on his decision in *Decibel*: "I just felt like a hypocrite hiding it, especially in the Christian music scene…. We *never* wanted to become associated with ignorance and intolerance."

6. Darby Crash

Born Jan Paul Beahm, the semi-closeted Germs singer burned out when he was just twenty-two years old, overdosing intentionally and cutting a promising career short.

7. Jobriath (aka "The True Fairy of Rock 'n' Roll")

Most people today don't know who Jobriath was, but damn. There wasn't a closet that could contain his fabulousness. He died of AIDS in 1983, one of the first music business casualties of the disease.

8. Samantha Ronson

This DJ/tabloid staple is better known for being Lindsay Lohan's ex and Mark Ronson's sis.

9. Tom Robinson

Though punk was full of activists, most of their causes did not benefit women or gays, and the scene contained a fair amount of homophobia. Robinson was one of the first out punks, making a splash with his anthem "Glad to Be Gay."

10. Daniela Sea

Though she's best known for her turn on *The L Word*, Sea also has a rich musical past having been part of Bitch and the Exciting Conclusion and the Gilman Street–based G'rups.

11. El Vez

The not exactly enlightened King probably takes a turn in his grave every time this self-proclaimed "Mexican Elvis" remakes one of his tunes.

12. Elton John

Was Elton really fooling anyone (besides his unfortunate ex-wife) with his whole "bisexual" phase? But it was a different world then and John was eventually honest with himself and the world at large when he came out. Though playing Rush Limbaugh's wedding and befriending known homophobe Eminem are certainly questionable antics for a gay dude.

13. Holly Johnson (Frankie Goes to Hollywood)

Johnson was the lead singer of Frankie Goes to Hollywood, but also made hits under his own name later. In 1993 he revealed that he was HIV-positive and in 1994, he released an autobiography, *A Bone in My Flute*. Though he plays music occasionally, Johnson's main concentration is painting these days.

14. Michael Stipe

For whatever reason, the REM front man was coy about his sexuality for many years. But lately he's mellowed and is often photographed with his long-term partner, the artist Thomas Dozol.

15. Jake Shears

A straight man could never get away with naming his band Scissor Sisters.

16. Rufus Wainwright

Son of Loudon Wainwright III and Kate McGarrigle, Wainwright is heir to a musical legacy that continues to evolve.

17. Pet Shop Boys

Neil Tennant and Chris Lowe formed PSB in 1982 and have sold over 100 million records (remember them?) worldwide. Their name does not have a lewd hamster connection as some frattish homophobes have suggested, but instead comes from two friends who worked in an Ealing, UK, pet shop.

18. Erasure

Like the Pet Shop Boys, Andy Bell and Vince Clarke perform theatrical, synth-poppy, dancey hits. One of their tours featured the boys riding out onstage atop a giant swan.

19. Bob Mould

If there's a genre that was more homophobic than heavy metal, it had to be hardcore. Which is probably why Hüsker Dü's Bob Mould kept his sexuality under wraps for so long.

20. Boy George

Oh, Boy.

21. KD Lang

Madonna once said of Lang, "Elvis is alive, and she's beautiful." The country crooner was pop's most high-profile lesbian for a long time, though now she's tired of being the poster girl for faux lesbian titillation. She told a reporter for the *Sunday Times*, "A friend of mine said we should go around 'inning' all the people who were acting gay."

22. George Michael

He wants your sex.

23. Melissa Etheridge

When Etheridge and her then-girlfriend Julie Cypher decided to have a baby, they looked to their friend group for sperm donors. Their pals included Bruce Springsteen, Al Gore, and a host of other high-profile candidates. Yet they chose David Crosby. Wouldn't a roll of the dice at a sperm bank have been a better option?

24. Joe Jackson

Just to be clear, we're talking about the "Steppin' Out" singer, not Michael Jackson's Little-Richard-on-a-bad-day-looking daddy.

25. Kele Okereke

The famously shy Bloc Party lead singer and rhythm guitarist came out in 2010 in an interview with *Butt* magazine. That same year he was dubbed Sexiest Out Gay Male Artist by LP33.com.

26. Jimmy Somerville (Bronski Beat)

Unlike many gays of a certain age, Somerville was lucky enough to have loving parents—something he never took for granted. Of his mom, he said, "She gave me loads of support. There were some friends of mine who told their parents and got thrown out.... One of my friends actually committed suicide because his parents threw him out. You need somebody to talk to, you need emotional support. You *don't* need someone telling you you're wrong." (*Rolling Stone*, Feb. 28, 1985)

27. Morrissey

For *decades* Morrissey has been claiming to be asexual, but it's fairly clear he's queer.

10 HIP–HOP SONGS RICH JUZWIAK MASTURBATED ALONG TO AS A TEENAGER IN THE EARLY '90S (P.S. HE'S GAY!)

As a teenager in the pre-Internet days, I had to take whatever porn I could find, and that mostly came in the form of soft-ish straight porn magazines. I tried to get into the tits but mostly found myself gravitating to reader mail columns like "Letters to *Penthouse*," wherein there was explicit mention of penises and what guys did with them. Around the same time, I began listening to hip-hop and would get turned on listening to the explicit sex talk that sometimes popped up on the truly hard-core albums. It wasn't a big jump to begin consuming that like porn. (Fun fact: I once interviewed Luther Campbell and characterized his explicit work as "porno rap." He said, "Porno rap? I've never heard it called that!" I was like, "Oh, maybe it was just me.") What's most interesting to me about all of this is that hip-hop didn't just satisfy a part of my nascent sexuality, but I was drawn to hip-hop in the first place for nonsexual reasons associated with being gay: I identified with the otherness of black people and black culture, because I, too, was part of a minority (mind you, none of this was conscious).

Anyway, I had a lot of the tracks below dubbed on one single mix, so that I didn't have to stop to change tapes. Clearly, I was priming myself for the ADHD-style porn consumption of the Internet. I'm happy to report that this stuff ultimately had little effect on me: Sure, I like black guys, but not more so than any other group and I only refer to a woman as a bitch on second reference, if at all.

1. "Findum, Fuckum, and Flee," NWA
Sample couplet: "Take a ticket to play with it like a Slinky / So put your lips on my big chocolate Twinkie."

2. "The Fuck Shop," 2 Live Crew
Sample couplet: "Now spread your wings open for the flight / Let me fill you up with something milky and white."

3. "Is the Pussy Still Good?," BWP
Sample couplet: "I'll swallow every ounce of that sticky cum / 'Cause that's how a dick suck should be done."

4. "On the Bone Again," Brooklyn Assault Team
Sample couplet: "Now I'm chillin', layin' on my bed / With my hand between my legs, playin' with my dick head…."

5. "Jerkit Circus," Digital Underground
Sample couplet: "Tonight he's gonna rock it with a whole new plan / He's got a date with his left hand."

6. "Tales from the Sexside," Choice
Sample couplet: "Now he has a face full / I raised up, asked could he breathe, he said, 'No, but it's tasteful!'"

7. "Froggy Style," Hi-C
Sample couplet: "I won't quit until my nuts are numb / I'm gonna hump your booty until I cum."

8. "Wide Open," LeShaun

Sample couplet: "Have you ever, ever, ever in your long-legged life / Have a sneaky, freaky finger make that butt feel so nice?"

9. "Woodchuck," Apache

Sample couplet: "Spread 'em (here they go) got 'em / The mission is to pound the pussy until I hit rock bottom."

10. "Menage a Trois Pt. II," Luke

Sample line: "Naw, that ain't cum, baby, that's something else that you may think it might be."

Rich Juzwiak runs the pop culture blog Four Four (fourfour.typepad.com) and cohosts "Pot Psychology," a web series on Jezebel.com. He is a regular contributor to the *Village Voice*, and has appeared on *This American Life*. In 2012, the book *Pot Psychology's How to Be: The Essential Guide to Life* will be published by Grand Central Publishing.

14 SUPAH–STAHS WHO LIKE THE POLE AND THE HOLE*

1. David Bowie

In her 1993 memoir, *Backstage Passes*, Bowie's bisexual ex-wife says the androgynous rocker "made a religion of slipping the Lance of Love into almost everyone around him," and intimated that the Thin White Duke once had it off with Mick Jagger (though Jagger and Bowie vehemently dispute this). After famously declaring his bisexuality in the '70s Bowie later lamented that his announcement was the biggest mistake he ever made. At least for puritanical American audiences. He's been married to Somalian supermodel Iman since 1992.

2. Iggy Pop

When you have a member as large and lovely as Mr. Pop's it's really not fair to limit yourself to schtupping just one gender, so, according to rumor, Iggy allegedly didn't. The film *Velvet Goldmine* told a heavily fictionalized version of the Iggy/Bowie love affair, but during the pre-AIDS, heroin-fueled days and nights of the '70s, it was all about boys who loved boys who loved girls who loved boys, so who cares? Iggy, however, disputes this, and in the book *The Story of Iggy Pop* talks about getting waylaid by a gay chapter of his fan club. "Once in a while, if I was like really asleep and they didn't think I was watching or anything they'd come and they'd try to pull on my nuts. I'd go, 'No, get off me! God, you boys.' But I liked them because they were culturally really aware and I dug that."

3. Elton John

Yes, yes, Elton John is now out and proud, but it took him a while (and a sham marriage to some sappy broad) to come out. The rhinestoned rocker started with baby steps, in 1976, telling a reporter for *Rolling Stone* magazine that he was bisexual. In 1989 he divorced his wife and announced he was now completely gay; in 2005 he married David Furnish. Thus far the twosome have been thwarted in their efforts to adopt a pair of orphans (one HIV-positive) from the Ukraine, but in 2011, they proudly showed off their brand new baby boy, born via surrogate. Unlike most celebrities who sell their baby pics to the highest bidders, John and Furnish donated all the proceeds from the sale of their photos to assorted children's charities.

4. Ani DiFranco

Righteous babe Ani DiFranco has always proudly declared herself bi and wrote love songs to both genders. But in 1998 she broke a million lesbian hearts when she married her male sound engineer; she did it again in 2009 when she married yet another dude after her first marriage went south.

5. Lou Reed

Though the crankiest man in rock has been shacked up with art-rocker Laurie Anderson for well over a decade (the two finally married in 2008), he used to stroll on the wild side quite regularly. In fact, his parents even committed him to a mental institution and subjected him to electroshock therapy hoping to jolt the gay out of him. It didn't take, and Reed never discriminated against bedmates by gender.

6. Janis Joplin

The '60s were such a weird, hypocritical time—sure, there were drugs, hours-long, noodling guitar jams, free love and all that, but hippie culture was ragingly sexist and pretty homophobic to boot. Which is probably why the woman that Leonard Cohen described "giving him head on the unmade bed" at the Chelsea Hotel wasn't exactly open about her sexuality. Joplin had sex with plenty of men, but, according to several sources, her most long-term relationship was with another woman.

7. Brett Anderson (Suede)

The fey rocker describes himself as "a bisexual man who never had a homosexual experience." But if you've never had a weiner anywhere near you, can you still claim bi-dom? Or, much like the sorority girl who makes out with another chick just for attention, are you just another boring straight co-opting the gay banner for a little bit of titillation cred? These questions are too deep to answer in one little book of lists, so we'll just leave it to you, the reader, to ponder.

8. Dave Davies

Long before the Gallagher brothers took over as rock's reigning family feud, there were the Kinks' Ray and Dave Davies. Davies' memoir, *Kink*, details the rock star's bisexuality and relationship with British blues singer Long John Baldry. In a 1996 interview, Davies explains, "There were a lot of people having bisexual relationships then. It was the time. You felt you could do, or at least try out, anything. It was all experimentation."

9. and 10. Howard Devoto and Pete Shelley (Buzzcocks)

The founders of Manchester's Buzzcocks are both openly bisexual. On the ambiguity of his solo song "Homosapien," Shelley explained to Pitchfork it was because "the object of my attention could be either. I can always say this one is about you, even if I wrote it about someone else."

11. Lady Gaga

Lady Gaga has earned her place as a gay icon, first as a wildly vocal supporter of the "Don't Ask, Don't Tell" repeal and again as a target for the Westboro Baptist Church, who changed their slogan "God Hates Fags" to "God Hates Gaga" for a string of 2010 concerts. Though most of her press involves her dating men, Gaga has declared herself bisexual and told *Rolling Stone* that her hit "Poker Face" was about feigning sexual pleasure with a man while dreaming of her mystery lady lover.

12. Brian Molko (Placebo)

Though he fathered a child with his longtime girlfriend, the androgynous, cosmetically inclined rock star was initially quite open about being into dudes too. He later regretted his openness, telling one interviewer, "Unfortunately, we became this faggy band in dresses in the eyes of the media. People started to talk about that and not the music as a by-product."

13. Billie Joe Armstrong

The Green Day singer has been married to a woman since the mid-'90s but had always told reporters he considered himself bisexual. This angered a lot of the band's more knuckleheaded fan base, much to his dismay. Armstrong noted, "There were a lot of people who didn't accept it, who were homophobic." These days he's less eager to classify himself as anything, saying his reluctance stems out of respect to his wife.

14. Gavin Rossdale

Mr. Gwen Stefani denied a youthful affair with cross-dressing British singer Marilyn for years, until he finally admitted it to a writer for *Details* magazine in 2010. Rossdale seems to have immediately regretted making the admission and allegedly begged the magazine to keep it out of the story because he didn't want to fess up to his wife.

HONORABLE MENTION

Imani the Misfit

The first time Imani busted a move on a guy, the dude pulled a knife and so Imani retreated back into the closet for a few years. Not anymore. Billing himself as Maryland's first bisexual porn-star rapper, Imani declares, "I'm a graphic designer and I take naked pictures. I've done three different masturbation videos. Another thing about me, I'm also anti-religious.... I got different videos—one is called 'Fuck the Bible'; another is called 'Fuck God.'"

DISHONORABLE MENTION

Pete Townshend

The Who's guitarist raised eyebrows when he confessed to journalist Timothy White that he knew how it felt to be a woman because he *was* a woman, and that "Rough Boys" was "almost a coming-out, an acknowledgment of the fact that I'd had a gay life and that I understood what gay sex was about." Danny Fields's memoir, which referred to Pete as one of his boyfriends for a time, angered the rocker and caused him to deny he'd ever *consciously* engaged in gay sex. Finally, in a 2002 interview with *Rolling Stone*, he copped to having experimented with guys in the '60s, but insisted he's a breeder through and through. Make up your mind, Pete.

* Allegedly!

41 OTHER NOTABLE BI GUYS AND GALS

1. Joan Baez
2. Alice Bag (the Bags)
3. Blu Cantrell
4. Vanessa Carlton
5. Nell Carter
6. Neneh Cherry
7. Sammy Davis Jr. (unconfirmed, but fun to imagine)
8. Marianne Faithfull
9. Fergie (the Black Eyed Pea, not the former princess)
10. Sia
11. Geri Halliwell (Spice Girls)
12. Debbie Harry
13. Sophie B. Hawkins
14. Nona Hendryx
15. Magdalen Hsu-Li
16. Grace Jones
17. Candye Kane
18. Les McKeown (Bay City Rollers)
19. Carmen McRae (jazz singer)
20. Mika
21. Nicki Minaj
22. Alanis Morrisette
23. Bif Naked
24. Laura Nyro
25. Sinéad O'Connor

26. Joan Osborne
27. Amanda Palmer
28. Peaches
29. Edith Piaf
30. Pink
31. Lisa Marie Presley (though she told Howard Stern she tries to keep that impulse "in check")
32. Dee Dee Ramone (though we're reluctant to count gay-for-pay)
33. Michelle Shocked
34. Skin (Skunk Anansie)
35. Bessie Smith
36. Jill Sobule
37. Dusty Springfield
38. Kinnie Starr
39. Steve Strange (Visage)
40. Corin Tucker
41. Kim Zolciak (Don't be tardy for *her* party.)

KURT B. REIGHLEY FINDS 10 SONGS THAT FLEW UNDER THE GAYDAR

Sometimes a song's homoerotic content is pretty obvious; neither Jill Sobule nor Katy Perry left much to the imagination when they released singles titled "I Kissed a Girl." Likewise, with an ever-increasing number of out-of-the-closet artists—ranging from old-guard favorites like Melissa Etheridge to rising stars such as Gossip and Scissor Sisters—enjoying commercial and critical success, the love that once dared not speak its name barely shuts up. But other ditties require listeners to read between the lines…or at least pay close attention to the lyrics. Here are ten tunes that can stand on their musical merit alone, but which also slipped queer-friendly content into impressionable young ears.

I. "You Don't Own Me," Lesley Gore
Like her '60s pop colleague Dusty Springfield, Gore ("It's My Party," "Judy's Turn to Cry") kept her sexual preference strictly under wraps at the height of her fame. Even

so, this 1962 number two hit was unusually defiant, warning suitors against trying to boss Lesley around. In light of her coming out in 2005, lyrics like "I'm free and I love to be free / To live my life the way I want / To say and do whatever I please" acquire a whole new resonance, especially in the rerecorded version showcased on Gore's comeback album, *Ever Since*.

2. "See My Friends," the Kinks

Five years before the Kinks scored a Top Ten smash on both sides of the pond by immortalizing the cross-dressing "Lola," Ray Davies penned this 1965 psychedelic UK hit about a gent who can't decide which way his garden gate swings. "It's about being a youth who is not quite sure of his sexuality," says the songwriter.

3. "John, I'm Only Dancing," David Bowie

On this non-LP single issued in 1972, our male narrator assures his disgruntled paramour John that, much as he digs a third party ("she turns me on"), their interaction on the dance floor is strictly platonic. Curiously, whether or not you read that pronoun "she" as referring to a male or female makes little difference; either way, Bowie is defending his flirtation to another dude.

4. "Rikki Don't Lose That Number," Steely Dan

Long before controversial troubadour Tom Robinson ("Glad to Be Gay") covered it in 1984, some savvy individuals "in the life" had decoded that Walter Becker and Don Fagen's 1974 Top Five tune was about a young man, new to the big city, making his first gay connection—and waffling about whether or not to take things further.

5. "53rd and 3rd," the Ramones

On this cut from the punk quartet's 1976 self-titled masterpiece, bassist Dee Dee Ramone recounts his misadventures as a hustler on what was at the time a notorious NYC block for picking up rent boys. At first he laments being passed over by the johns, but when he does find a client, the encounter takes an ugly turn, with the deeply conflicted narrator graduating from prostitution to murder in just a few chord changes.

6. "Ever Fallen in Love With Someone (You Shouldn't've Fallen in Love With)," the Buzzcocks

Of course you have. We all do. But when the songwriter is bisexual Pete Shelley, the possibilities get tangled. Shelley's 1981 debut solo single, "Homosapien," actually earned a BBC ban for what the morality police decreed was its obvious celebration

of gay sex—but as early as 1978, the Buzzcocks' "Ever Fallen in Love . . .," in which Pete laments that "if I start a commotion / I'll only end up losing you," was already getting the raised eyebrow from queer fans.

7. "Rough Boys," Pete Townshend

For years, Townshend dodged is-he-or-isn't-he inquiries, waiting until 2002 to admit that, aside from some same-sex experimentation, he identified as heterosexual. Nevertheless, this satire of UK punk culture, featuring exhortations like "Tough boys / Come over here / I wanna bite and kiss you," still carries a potent whiff of homoeroticism. That fact that some listeners misheard the lyric "I'm gonna get inside your bitter mind" as "I'm gonna get inside *your bed or mine*" didn't help matters.

8. "Kid," the Pretenders

Chrissie Hynde's lyric on this gem from the band's eponymous 1980 album is pretty open-ended. It can easily be read as one side of a difficult conversation with a child or loved one. But factor in lines like "You think it's wrong / I can tell you do," and it isn't hard to understand why many queer men and women choose to interpret it as a coming-out tale turned sour.

9. "Rent," Pet Shop Boys

It seems impossible to fathom today, but Pet Shop Boys' Neil Tennant didn't officially come out until 1994. Yeah. But you didn't need a degree in gender studies to decipher this cut from the duo's 1987 album, *Actually*. Forget the fact that "rent boy" is British slang for a male prostitute—the pair also rerecorded this song about being kept by a wealthy lover on Liza Minnelli's *Results* album. It doesn't get much gayer than that, folks.

10. "Michael," Franz Ferdinand

On their 2004 debut, the hottest Scottish musical export since the Bay City Rollers snuck in this hip-shaker, on which singer Alex Kapranos praised getting whisker burn from "the only one I'd ever want." Inspired by watching two male friends hook up at a Glasgow nightclub, Kapranos—who is heterosexual—told the *Advocate*, "It's more about sexual yearning and passion on a physical level" than a love song.

Kurt B. Reighley, aka DJ El Toro, is a Seattle-based author (*United States of Americana*), entertainer, and radio host on KEXP.

NORMAN BRANNON'S 5 REASONS HARDCORE IS MORE HOMOEROTIC THAN EMO

From the perspective of a gay man who went to his first hardcore punk show in 1987 as a closeted teenager, the subtext of male desire in what is an unquestionably hypermasculine subculture was kind of a no-brainer. It was also, however, a major social conflict: America in the 1980s was rife with homophobia, which—as if it weren't widespread enough already—had arguably reached a cultural nadir with the emergence of AIDS and the incessant moral politicking of Ronald Reagan and the Moral Majority. Because the hardcore scene did not live inside the imagined force field that we believed separated "us" from "them," this conflict seeped into our own discourse: In spite of our self-proclaimed rebellion, hardcore kids adopted some of mainstream America's so-called moral values and enforced them with violent rhetoric and, in some cases, violent action.

A few years later, in the early to mid-1990s, many of us who were feeling alienated from this aesthetic began making music that reflected a more melodic sensibility; it was a lot less angry, and a little more angsty. My own band engaged with a variety of *feelings*—not the least of which was vulnerability —and this made some traditional hardcore purists rather uncomfortable. We were feminizing punk rock, they argued. It was hardcore for nerds, they said. One fundamentalist hardcore group actually name-checked my band for a song they called "Texas Is the Reason That Emo Sucks." Before long, this word *emo*—which had been fashioned from an insult hurled at a handful of Washington, D.C., bands in the '80s—had begun to develop a more colloquial meaning: It suggested that you were soft, weak, delicate, and defective. It implied *gayness*.

This is, to be polite, terribly ironic.

I. Hardcore bands sing almost exclusively for and about men.

You can say what you want about a band called Cute Is What We Aim For, but there is very little doubt that "The Curse of Curves" refers to a woman's body. And when it comes to asserting your sexuality, there is probably nothing more brazen than naming your band Boys Like Girls. Which makes it all the more glaring to note the total omission of similar sentiments from the male-obsessed hardcore scene. I mean, there doesn't seem to be *a single girl* in the DYS "Wolfpack" (where "every kid is my brother here"), and Judge's "New York Crew"—which repeatedly invokes the nostalgia of a "New York brotherhood"—almost makes 1982 sound like a fraternal S&M club. At the very least, I can't imagine wearing "chains around our waists" anywhere else.

2. The hardcore scene values the gym-fit male body.

I always found that Youth of Today lyric about being "physically strong and morally straight" kind of funny; the fact that Ray Cappo basically cribbed these lines from the Boy Scout oath should tell you something about its intended audience. Of course, the archetype of the clean-cut, worked-out hardcore kid is just not that far removed from the image of the gym-bodied Chelsea boy that has dominated our gay male physical standards for the last twenty-five years. If anything, the skinny emo look has become an increasingly *heterosexual* cultural image, while hardcore's curious interest in the sculpted male physique persists to this day: When a quick search of the popular hardcore Internet message board hosted by Bridge Nine Records pulls up *a 458-page thread* dedicated to "Bodybuilding and Fitness," there can be no uncertainty that the male body continues to inspire great fascination among the genre's ranks.

3. There could never be an emo song called "Pay to Cum."

Because of the fact that the male/female ratio at a hardcore show is so disproportionate to that of even an emo concert, we have to understand that the rhetoric associated with each genre is going to be radically different from the other. So despite the fact that "Pay to Cum" has very little to do with actual "cum," the Bad Brains chose this line as the dominant imagery for this song because ejaculation is part of the language of male bonding. In other words, we can safely assume that the male/female ratio of people who have *actually* "paid to cum" is going to be equally as disproportionate as the dichotomy between genders at a Bad Brains show. H.R. might as well have said, "No big deal, dude. It's just us guys tonight."

4. There is no greater homoerotic ritual than the mosh pit.

It's one of those things that seems obvious to everyone except those who participate, but there is an almost Greek sense of androcentrism about the mosh pit that is rivaled by almost no other modern-day expression of physicality between men. On one level, it is an expression of masculinity itself—or, as SS Decontrol once sang, "Think we're pussies afraid to fight / Then enter our pit and feel our might." But deeper than that, it's a safe space where men can press their sweaty torsos against each other, where strong and agile male bodies are freely admired, and where men can express their physical affection for each other in a way that both affirms their manhood and actually allows for the male gaze to be projected upon each other. Frankly, I've seen gay porn that was less sensual than some of the things I've experienced at CBGB.

5. The lady doth protest too much.

In what is most likely the most heteronormative example of '80s hardcore, Kraut's Davey Gunner dedicates an entire song to "fucking my girl at the matinee"—to which emo's closest successor is the Starting Line's "Bedroom Talk," where singer Kenny Vasoli announces he's "gonna tear your ass up like we just got married." There is no doubt that both songs convey patriarchy—the woman in "Matinee" is repeatedly described as "*my* girl" and Vasoli's woman is "all *mine* now," both denoting ownership—but only Kraut transmit an image in which the male is both subject *and* object: Whereas a woman's body is the unambiguous locus of desire in "Bedroom Talk," the privileged image in "Matinee" is that of having one's dick sucked—making the girl in this song more of a phantasm than a sexual being. Although the woman is intended to be a signifier of Gunner's heterosexuality, she is *still* relegated to the background of his male phallus.

It shouldn't be too surprising, then, that even when hardcore songs are trying to be explicitly homophobic, the results *still* teem with a kind of homoeroticism that simply doesn't exist in emo. This a scene that spawned a band called the Circle Jerks and a song called "Tooling for Anus." It's the scene that inspired Iron Cross, whose debut EP features both a song about a skinhead who kills a gay man and suggestive lyrics like "You don't know how it feels to put the boot in!" It's a scene in which an anti-gay Bad Brains song actually uses the term "fudge buns" as a euphemism for gay sex.

It could be that, someday, these instances of homoerotic imagery and ritual will be appreciated as positive expressions of a confused adolescence. And I'd like to think that, at some point, hardcore's social rebellion will finally extend itself to the dismissal of institutionalized notions of gender. But until then, it's impossible to skirt this genre's unique and seemingly unconscious entanglement with male desire. Because, really, it should probably go without saying that anyone who thinks about gay sex long enough to create nonsensical euphemisms for gay sex most likely thinks about gay sex way more than the guy from Dashboard Confessional.

Norman Brannon is a pop critic, musician, and author who most famously expressed his pre-millennium tension as the guitar player for Shelter and Texas Is the Reason. He currently lives in New York City and writes at Nervousacid.org.

6 SHITTY HOMOPHOBIC MOMENTS IN ROCK

1. Kings of Leon drummer Nathan Followill gets his manties in a bunch after *Glee* creator Ryan Murphy complains about the band's refusal to let the show use their music. Followill tweeted: "Dear Ryan Murphy, let it go. See a therapist, get a manicure, buy a new bra. Zip your lip and focus on educating 7yr olds how to say fuck."

2. In 1990, Skid Row's Sebastian Bach is photographed wearing a T-shirt that reads "AIDS Kills Fags Dead." After initially treating the outrage as a joke, Bach later apologized and started wearing a T-shirt that read "AIDS Kills Everyone."

3. Slayer guitarist Kerry King is apparently afraid of tiny, enclosed spaces where homosexuals might linger. He told one reporter, "If you're a gay person I'd rather not be stuck in a lift with you." (Confidential to Kerry King: I've seen what you look like and I don't think you have much to worry about from either gender.)

4. There is so much homophobic badness coming out of Slim Shady's mouth at any given time, it's hard to limit it to just one. So we picked this gem that he shared with a reporter from Kronick.com, complaining about all the grief he's caught for being a gay-hater. "Nobody would say shit if I didn't say somethin' about homosexuals. But as soon as you talk about homosexuals, gay people are really uptight I guess."

5. This is rich coming from a man who wears shiny purple suits, high heels, and more product than Little Richard, but Prince told a reporter for the *New Yorker*, "You've got the Republicans, and basically they want to live according to [the Bible]. But there's the problem of interpretation, and you've got some churches, some people, basically doing things and saying it comes from here, but it doesn't. And then on the opposite end of the spectrum you've got blue, you've got the Democrats, and they're, like, 'You can do whatever you want.' Gay marriage, whatever. But neither of them is right." (Though in his defense, Prince did later claim he was misquoted.)

6. Between his repulsive song about murdering gay men by pouring acid over them and then being arrested with a group of friends for viciously assaulting men they suspected of homosexuality, reggae star Buju Banton is the poster boy for homophobia. Not that it needed a poster. In a rare instance of karma (or just extreme stupidity), Banton was arrested for trying to purchase a large quantity of cocaine from an undercover cop. He was awaiting trial as this book went to press.

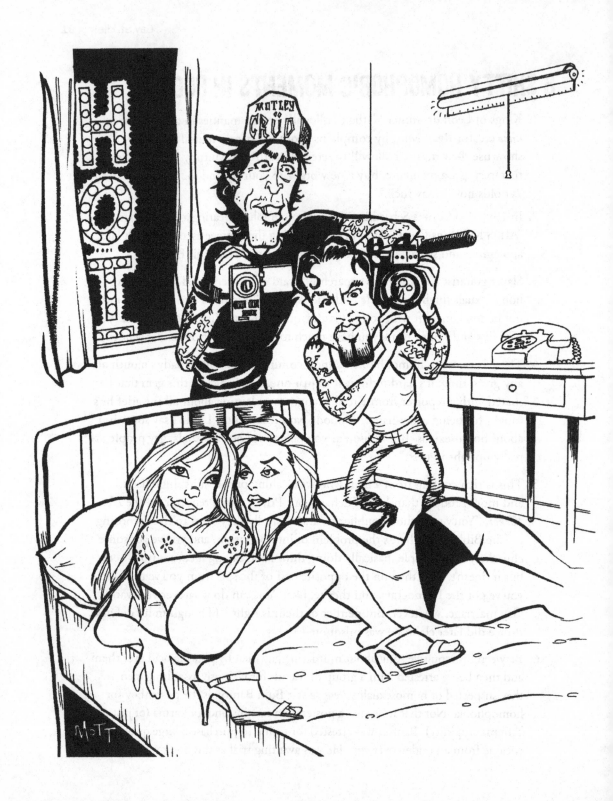

GIRLS (AND BOYS) ON FILM

6

MIKE MCPADDEN'S 10 BEST ROCK 'N' ROLL PORNOS

Sticks and skins. Stacks and power chords. Fuzz boxes and solid bodies. The realms of rock music and sex films emerge from the same primordial place and often deliver the same spine-crackling, mind-spinning, soul-exploding delights…when done right, of course. The following list compiles ten top-ticket fusions of heavy jams and heavier jamming. So come. Get your rocks off.

1. Pam and Tommy Lee: *Stolen Honeymoon* (1998)

Director: Tommy Lee
Cast: Pamela Anderson, Tommy Lee
In purely pornographic terms, *Stolen Honeymoon* is no earth-shaker: Onboard a tacky boat, a fake-boobed blonde gets power-dorked by a tattooed goofball. History gets made, however, when one considers that the Formica funbags belong to the world's premier blonde bombshell at the height of her hormonal planetary conquest and that the meat-anchor is attached to heavy metal's (then) highest-profile car crash of a drummer. For retro-context, think of Marilyn Monroe mounting Keith Moon or Farrah Fawcett getting harpooned by John Bonham's Moby-Dick.

2. *New Wave Hookers* (1985)

Director: Gregory Dark
Cast: Traci Lords, Brooke Fields, Desiree Lane, Jack Baker, Jamie Gillis
From the opening strains of "Electrify Me" by Mexi-punks the Plugz, the Dark Brothers' *New Wave Hookers* pushed the final days of theatrical porn into a frenzy of Day-Glo outrage and neon nihilism. Jamie Gillis and Jack Baker (who, yes, really did portray drummer "Sticks" on Happy Days) literally dream of running an escort service specializing in "new wave bitches." Among their fantasy figures is devil-horned Traci Lords. Iggy Pop once opined that "thirteen-year-old girls" powered rock-n-roll. Traci is fifteen here. Close enough.

3. *Circa '82* (2008)

Director: Dave Naz
Cast: Sasha Grey, Ashley Blue, Madison Young, Keith Morris
One-upping (or is that 82-upping?) contemporary "alt-porn" directors like the puckishly, punkishly named Eon McKai, erotic photographer Dave Naz chronicles the comings and more comings of L.A. youth during the era of the first *Decline of Western Civilization*, complete with a Circle Jerks soundtrack. Head Jerk Keith Morris appears, as does ex-Germ Don Bolles. Compounding the porn-rock pedigree: Naz played in Chemical People, which provided killer theme songs to Dark Brothers classics such as *Black Throat* (which was later covered by NYC's naked-lady-fronted transgressors Boss Hog).

4. *Nightdreams* (1981)

Director: Rinse Dream (Stephen Sayadian)
Cast: Dorothy LeMay, Loni Sanders, Jacqueline Lorians
Writer-director team Stephen Sayadian and Jerry Stahl most famously vaporized the barrier between the stroke house and the art house with their post-nuke avant-porn *Café Flesh* (1982), but their initial outing, *Nightdreams*, is surreal freak-out equally adept at blowing minds and laps alike. Dorothy LeMay submits to mind probes at a mental clinic, and among the visions she shows us are a trio of lesbian cowgirls licking buttholes to a cover of Johnny Cash's "Ring of Fire" by Wall of Voodoo (*si*, they of "Mexican Radio" fame). Tongues burrow into bungs in perfect rhythm to the cries of "It burns! Burns! Burns!" rendering *Nightdreams* all wet, in the best sense.

5. *Broken* (2007)

Director: Dave Navarro
Cast: Sasha Grey, Jenna Haze, Evan Seinfeld (from Biohazard)
Jane's Addiction guitarist Dave Navarro follows up his post-Lollapalooza gigs as a reality TV show subject (*Carmen and Dave: An MTV Love Story*) and reality TV game show host (*Rock Star: Supernova*) by directing fluffy-muffed Sasha Grey in a high-gloss sex video. Some couplings are rough, some are rote, and all are doused in pretension that's occasionally laughable, but most often boring. In short: Dave Navarro smut is exactly like Dave Navarro music (I did like that game show, though).

6. *Teenage Cruisers* (1977)

Director: Johnny Legend
Cast: Serena, Christine Shaffer, John Holmes
"Fee-fee-fi / Fo-fo-fum / I smell pussy / And I want some!" So goes *Teenage Cruisers'* titular rave-up performed by Rasputin-bearded rockabilly roughneck Johnny Legend in his one and only X-rated directorial effort. Comedy bits connect the sex parts while '50s-style guitar mayhem wails throughout. Featured artists include X's Billy Zoom, Ray Campi, Jerry Sikorski, and Alvis Wayne. Rhino Records put out the soundtrack album.

7. *Backstage Girls* (2008)

Director: Uncredited
Cast: Elexis, Darryl Hanah, Joelean, Ginger Lee
Real-life all-lesbian semi-metal outfit Kill Slowly supplies the sound and the setting for this strictly sapphic sextravaganza. Guitarist Lily Paige even gets in on the tits-and-ax action, gobbling groupie gash belonging to Elexis Monroe and Bobbi Starr. As with all other Girlfriends Films productions, the bodies here are natural, the sex comes off as real and, in this case, everything rocks in a more literal than usual fashion.

8. *Jimi Hendrix: The Sex Tape* (196?)

Director: Unknown
Cast: Jimi Hendrix, a couple of hippie chicks
Discovered in a trunk bearing the title *Black Man*, *The Jimi Hendrix Sex Tape* features what does appear to be the guitar god diddling and fiddling with a pale pair of electric ladies. It runs eleven minutes. The remainder of this Vivid release is typical '60s reminiscing from the likes of career rock-star-fluid siphons Cynthia Plaster Caster and Pamela Des Barres.

9. *Punk Rock,* aka *Teenage Runaways* (1977)

Director: Carter Stevens
Cast: Susaye London, Crystal Sync, Jean Sanders, Wade Nichols
A impressively scuzzy private dick saga regarding a teenage sex slavery ring run out of Max's Kansas City(!) is made eminently more remarkable by its actually being released in two pointedly different versions: one a full-penetration XXX film noir, the other an R-rated punksploitation music showcase for local NYC acts the Fast, the Squirrels, and Spicy Bits. Director Carter Stevens first sought out Debbie Harry for the lead. He didn't get her.

10. *John Wayne Bobbitt Uncut* (1994)

Director: Ron Jeremy
Cast: John Wayne Bobbitt, Veronica Brazil, Letha Weapons, Vince Neil, Lemmy Kilmister
The very first example of the modern era's "celebreality" porn is as ripped from the headlines as the subject matter's sex organ was ripped from its crotch-socket. John Wayne Bobbit plays (with) himself while Veronica Brazil portrays his hotheaded, knife-wielding wife Lorena, who notoriously severed Bobbit's bobbler in 1993. Motörhead madman Lemmy Kilmister discovers the tossed-out tallywacker and Mötley Crüe's Vince Neil turns up as a bartender. A sequel, *Frankenpenis*, features no rock stars and bombed.

11. *Phallusifer: The Immoral Code* (2006)

Director: Harlot Queen
Cast: Harlot Queen, black metal dude
Phallusifer insists on letting you know it's the first-ever "black metal porn film" and, if we were to judge the genre based solely on this 65-minute S&M-tinged "Satanic" genital bout between skinny dom Harlot Queen and an even skinnier no-name longhair, even the horniest of corpse-painted Venom and Mayhem boosters would not fret if it were to be the last. Alas, black metal perverts should rather look to top what Phallusifer has to offer. It, like the viewer, will not be hard.

Mike McPadden is the head writer of MrSkin.com. He is all other things to all other comers at McBeardo.com.

14 BANDS NAMED AFTER PORN STARS OR XX FLICKS

I. Alexisonfire
Named after lactating porn star Alexis Fire, the band added the "on" after the juicy jezebel objected.

2. Cinderella
This hair metal band was inspired by the soft-core version of the fairy tale. *Pfft*.

3. Fastball
If you're going to name yourselves after a porno flick, at least pick one with an appealing name. Note: When it comes to fucking, faster isn't always better.

4. Faster Pussycat
While not exactly X-rated, the Russ Meyer classic for which this band is named did feature a whole lot of boobie action and the babealicious Tura Satana.

5. Ginger Lynn
Adult Video News named Ms. Lynn number seven on their list of the fifty greatest porn stars of all time. Unfortunately, her long-haired namesakes aren't on anyone's Top Ten list.

6. Lord Tracy
Traci Lords wouldn't let them use her name so they just transposed it and changed the spelling. *Verrry* tricky.

7. Mr. Bungle
Happy accident that there's also a character called Mr. Bungle in a '70s porno?

8. New Pornographers
The band that spawned Neko Case was thought to be named for Jimmy Swaggart's proclamation that music was the "new pornography," but that came after they got together. So perhaps they inspired Swaggart.

9. Poets and Porn Stars

Claim to fame: They made it onto an episode of *Californication*.

10. Porn on the Cob

One word: corny.

11. Pornflakes

Never made it big outta Baltimore, and broke up in the '90s, but what a great name.

12. Porno for Pyros

Inspired not by on-screen rutting, Perry Farrell's post–Jane's Addiction band instead got its name from the televised riots and fires set after the Rodney King verdict.

13. Roger's Porn Collection

This Austin-based hardcore band does actually have someone named Roger (Racho) in the band, which leads one to believe they're named after his used stack of sticky mags.

14. Tit Pig

This Seattle-based band's namesake is buff, über-macho gay porn star Steve Hurley, who—by the looks of things—could kick these ironic art school boys' asses, but(t) hard.

GROUPIES  7

CYNTHIA PLASTER CASTER'S
8 MOST INTERESTING COCKS IN ROCK

1. Wayne Kramer
Poor Wayne Kramer, everyone who's seen it thinks he has a small penis, but he only got the head of his dick in there. He was up against a wall of hard alginate [the stuff dental molds are made from]. But he doesn't have a small dick at all.

2. Jimi Hendrix
Now *that* was an unbelievable night. We were the first ones to make it to his hotel after he played his first show. When I popped the question, he said he'd heard about me from somewhere in the cosmos—he was really mellow and groovy. "Come on up to the hotel and let's do it."

We couldn't believe we were riding in an elevator with the band instead of climbing the fire escape. It was one of my first castings and so because of that I didn't know to lubricate his pubes. So once it cast, he was stuck in it. Jimi Hendrix wearing nothing but his gaucho hat and some kind of panne velvet top…. It took me fifteen minutes to pull his pubes out. I let it sit for three days. When I finally took it out, it was in three pieces: head, shaft, and balls. I stuck it together with Elmer's glue.

3. Aynsley Dunbar (drummer for Frank Zappa, John Mayall, Jefferson Starship and many others)

He wouldn't dip unless he felt he was up to full capability. I wasted about three or four different molds waiting for him to get there. He may have finally penetrated on try number four.

4. David Yow (Jesus Lizard)

He was up to such full capability that we couldn't get him out of the mold! The head just wouldn't shrink.

5. Momus

Rumored to have the biggest cock in Britain, he could never get hard enough to get a good mold. So we had to work with what we had.

6. Clint Poppie/Clint Mansell (from Pop Will Eat Itself)

His came out twisted, like a pig's tail. The hardening alginate pushes down the penis—which is why so many of them look shorter than they were. When you have a long, curved dick, it gets pushed down in a circular pattern. I love when it happens. He didn't like it, though.

7. Chris Connelly (Revolting Cocks)

Chris is anything but revolting; he's a real sweetheart and beautifully endowed. His cock was like the Bermuda Triangle, though. On three different occasions the mold failed. It got to the point where his girlfriend thought I was doing it on purpose so I could see more of his dick.

8. Lawrence Barraclough

Not a musician, but he was the smallest—it was like a thimble. He made a documentary about living with a very small penis, called "My Penis and Everyone Else's."

Cynthia Plaster Caster is a recovering groupie and former Chicago mayoral candidate who makes plaster casts of penises and breasts. Visit her at www.cynthiaplastercaster.com.

WHERE WOULD ROCK BE WITHOUT SLUTTY DAMES? 11 BANDS NAMED FOR LADIES OF DUBIOUS MORALITY

1. Barenaked Ladies
2. Barnyard Slut
3. Cycle Sluts from Hell
4. Gigolo Aunts
5. GTO's
6. Joy Division
7. Nicky Shitz and the Slutty Nuns
8. Sisters of Mercy
9. Slut Sister
10. Splatterwhore
11. Whore du Jour

12 ROCKERS TALK ABOUT GROUPIES . . .

1. Violent J (Insane Clown Posse)
"I'm banging this chick and I got the condom on it. I bust a load in the condom and the condom fills up and after I pull my ding-a-ling out and she says, 'Fuck that, I want something.' So you know what she does? She pulls the condom off my dick and sucks the nut out of the condom…puts it in her little purse and walks away." (Interview with *Backstage Pass*)

2. Marilyn Manson (talking about an incident with Trent Reznor)
"[W]e ended up finding…a mysterious nodule—maybe it was white fuzz or a piece of corn—that she had on the outer region of her rectum. It horrified us and we looked at each other with disgust and shock. But we knew that we must continue with our debasement of this poor unsuspecting person. So I found a cigarette lighter, and I started to burn her pubic hair. Though it didn't hurt her, it didn't help things smell any better than they already did." (*The Long Hard Road Out of Hell*)

3. Keith Richards
"There were loads of groupies out there that were just good old girls who liked to take care of guys. Very mothering in a way. And if things got down to that, okay, maybe go to bed and have a fuck. But it wasn't the main thing with groupies and most of them were not particularly attractive." (*Life*)

4. Dom
"After the show we were all just hanging out with Ratatat and this pregnant woman walked over to Erik and just sprayed her breast milk all over his face. This is the god's honest truth. And then her husband came over, and high-fived him, like, 'Yeah, my wife just breastmilked [sic] a rock star!' That is definitely the strangest thing that has ever happened…thus far." (From an interview on Pitchfork.com, Jan. 12, 2010)

5. Michael Lardie (Great White)
"I don't think women should be barefoot and pregnant. So it's interesting what happens when the young ladies of Salt Lake come to a concert. Everyone's real open about sex, like 'Yeah, this is what we're here for.'" (*Spin*, Aug. 1990)

6. Lemmy, talking about Jimi Hendrix

"I've never seen a snake for chicks like that guy. Chicks just went nuts for him. He'd just sort of look at them and smile, and go 'Whatcha looking at?' It'd be crass on anyone else, but with him it just worked 'cos he looked like sex incarnate. And there was a lotta sex about 'cos they gave us acid and the contraceptive pill in the same year." (SabotageTimes.com, Dec. 23, 2010)

7. Jay-Z

"Detroit...got the best pussy. They just straight 'bout it. I respect that more than somebody who tries to front. I'm in town for one night. What the fuck I need with a girl with a value?" (*Vibe*, Aug. 1999)

8. Roddy Bottum (Faith No More and Imperial Teen), bemoaning the lack of male groupies

"I was looking forward to just the concept, a different take on the girl-groupie stereotype. But it hasn't really happened." (*Advocate*, Feb. 16, 1999)

9. DJ Whoo Kid

"All they have to do is walk around the corner with a tight skirt and a perverted artist will be lured into the moisture." (MissLS.net)

10. Julian Casablancas (the Strokes)

"It's funny, though, because although we really like girls, it's almost as if we like each other better. We'll definitely go get laid, but we won't hang out with the girl and be like, 'Oh, I love you,' we'll go straight back to the band." (*NME*, 2001)

11. Kid Rock

"Europeans don't seem to have the groupie mentality. In America, there are nude girls in the audience. At every show there are nude girls in the audience." (NYRock.com)

12. Robert Plant

"One minute she's twelve and the next minute she's thirteen and over the top. Such a shame. They haven't got the style that they had in the old days...way back in '68." (*Rolling Stone*, Mar. 13, 1975)

...AND 10 GROUPIES TALK ABOUT MEN

1. Über-groupie "Sweet Connie" Hamzy
"And who comes into the back lounge? *Neil fucking Diamond*...Neil looks me up and down and nods his approval. Then he gets high with us and disappears backstage. A few minutes later, his manager says he wants to see me in his dressing room. So I knock on the door, and there's Neil waiting for me in a blue robe. And I didn't just suck him—there was fucking, too." (*Spin*, Jan. 2005)

2. Ex-groupie Jessica Shoaf expounding on the less-glam aspects of groupiedom
"A lot of them can be assholes. It's like messing around with chicks is something to do because they're bored and out of town, so it's like, 'Let's bring her on the bus and stick drumsticks up her ass.'" (*Spin*, 12/02)

3. Cherry Vanilla, ex-groupie, Warhol Superstar, author of *Lick Me: How I Became Cherry Vanilla*
"[Being a groupie] is probably the purest holiest thing in rock and roll. The groupie is the one person in the music industry—the *only* person—there to give, not get. It's very pure...very non-monetary. Just showing your passion for the music and appreciation for what these guys go through. I'm trying to make the word *groupie* be a positive word, not a negative. I'm fine with it; call me a groupie." (interview with the author)

4. Courtney Love talking to Pamela Des Barres
"I *wanted* to be a groupie, but I wasn't really pretty enough. There is one heavy metal rock star I slept with. It's a fairly well known fact, but I can't tell you who it was. It's so goddamn embarrassing. So yeah, I did score once in my yellow tube top and my red painter pants. [*Laughs.*] Back then there was this girl that I would hang out with who was pretty bottom of the barrel. She could never really get past the road manager. And when she did she would get to, like, drummers. To me the whole thing was, 'Is this your dream? That this guy is going to fall in love with you and take you away and marry you?'" (PamelaDesBarres.com, Mar. 1994)

5. Pamela Des Barres
"You know what rock 'n' roll means, right? It means rock 'n' roll in the sack. It means sex: the lyrics, the beat of it, the thunderous feeling through your body.

Before the word *groupie* even existed I knew that I wanted to share myself with someone who created that music and turned me on in every kind of way." (*Independent*, Sept. 23, 2007)

6. Tura Satana, movie star/groupie/badass

"Elvis [Presley] kissed like a fish. Frank [Sinatra] was built like a studhorse and he knew what he was doing." (*Time Out Chicago*, Oct. 23–29, 2008)

7. Bebe Buell, model/musician/groupie

"It's scary what Elvis [Costello] does. He writes these lyrics because he knows I will see them, but he also knows that if I try to express this to people, they will think I am nuts. He wants people to think I'm crazy; it delights him. *But deep down he knows the truth.*" (*Is Tiny Dancer Really Elton's Little John?: Music's Most Enduring Mysteries, Myths, and Rumors Revealed*, Gavin Edwards)

8. Karrine "Superhead" Steffans, groupie/author

"I'm a genius. I'm a genius. I think that I've developed a product that people want, it's supply and demand and I'm obviously good at that thus far. So thank God for that." (BlackVoices.com, Apr. 16, 2009)

9. Alycen Rowse, describing the night John Entwistle died (in bed with her!)

"The thing about the night with John and the morning after, mind you, which is when the shit hit the fan so to speak, is if it was anybody else they probably would have stolen stuff out of that room, gone straight to the press, and made a big debacle about it. I was seventeen years into my groupie life at the time, so I was so integrated into the rock 'n' roll family. I don't want this to sound egotistical, but he couldn't have gone with a better woman, because I know how to keep the privacy. I didn't even think about touching anything in the room, except for the body and doing mouth-to-mouth." (GlideMagazine.com, Oct. 4, 2010)

10. Roxana Shirazi, groupie turned author

"I was always more into Nikki Sixx. But when we went to dinner, I found him a little dull. He talked about his gardening." (*The Last Living Slut: Born in Iran, Bred Backstage*)

PRINCESS SUPERSTAR'S 7 MISTAKES GUYS MAKE WHEN TRYING TO PICK UP THE TALENT

1. Ask for an autograph first. That just puts us on a different playing field and then I am not gonna think you are hot. Besides, did you know 90 percent of autographs are lost/thrown away in the first week after getting them? It's just a weird practice.

2. Be completely wasted. There is nothing uglier than that. Eyes bulging out, not focusing, totally disheveled and stinky. Yumm, let me hit that!

3. Tell me how much you love my two most popular songs that I've done. At least pick out some of my obscure material if you want to flatter me.

4. See if I want to go eat McDonald's or something like that after the show. Duh, I am a vegan. If you want to pick me up (or any girl for that matter) do some research before you invite me out.

5. Be taking a million pictures of me when I am performing (unless that is your job) and always in my face when I am performing. Girls prefer mystery.

6. Treat anybody arrogantly—like security or another fan—in front of me.

7. If you see that the talent has a boyfriend and he is there, don't even try it. Actually if you *know* the talent has a boyfriend (or again, any girl you like for that matter), it is good moral practice to leave her alone. There are plenty of fish in the sea. Being a "star" does not make the girl better than any other girl (in fact, usually we are more cuckoo!).

Princess Superstar (aka Concetta Kirschner) gets her first taste of music from her parents' daily servings of '70s soul and rock in the suburbs of Philadelphia. At the ripe young age of seventeen, Superstar packed her belongings, moved to New York City, and restarted her life as an international DJ/rap sensation, collaborating with everyone from Moby to Kool Keith to the Prodigy. You can find her online at PrincessSuperstar.com.

ERIC DAVIDSON'S 5 MOST FREQUENT GROUPIE QUOTES . . .

1. "You don't remember me, do you? Asshole!"
2. [Sigh] "It's Jenny!"
3. "I don't really do hard drugs." [Sip, sip sip, gulp . . .]
4. "It's okay...it's okay. We were drinking a lot. Let's just try to go to sleep."
5. "I'm on Facebook too. Call me...[under her breath] asshole."

...AND HIS 5 MOST FREQUENT RESPONSES TO SAID GROUPIE

1. "Oh, hey. Wow, you look great!"

2. "Right, right, Jenny. Yeah, what's up?"

3. "No, you're thinking of coke. This is vodka."

4. "Fuck, man, tours are just so stressful, y'know?"

5. "Yeah, damn, I think I dropped it in the toilet last night. It's not really working. Fuck, tours are so stressful, y'know?"

Eric Davidson is the front man for longtime Columbus, Ohio, punk band New Bomb Turks and a freelance rock journalist who has written and edited for the *Village Voice*, the *Cleveland Scene*, the *San Francisco Bay Guardian*, and *CMJ*, among many publications. He recently wrote his first book, *We Never Learn: The Gunk Punk Undergut 1988–2001* (Backbeat Books), which chronicles the international garage-punk scene of the '90s. He currently lives in Brooklyn, New York.

LOVE AND MARRIAGE

COCO'S 8 RULES FOR KEEPING YOUR RAPPER HAPPY

1. You must love his music the most! Never become distracted by a pop hit while you're listening to his new song on the radio!

2. Remember when you first met your honey for the first time? You were more than likely looking sexy—high heels, miniskirt, stockings, booty shorts—whatever! *That*'s the girl he went after! Don't become a bum. Do not ever lose that look!

3. Find out his favorite drinks, foods, or meals—like Kool-Aid, chili dogs, tacos, etc. Become an expert in their preparation.

4. Even though rappers like to boast about money, show him you respect the value of a dollar. Nobody likes a spend-crazy, wasteful, high-maintenance bitch.

5. He may have hobbies that you think are stupid (XBox, sports, etc.). Let him indulge in them and support his interests—like video games, for example. Hey, at least you know where he is!

6. Learn to get your point across as quickly and directly as possible. Men don't like to talk too much. Too many words all the time and he'll shut you out and you will drive him away.

7. You need to be the best sexual partner he's ever had in his life! Figure out what you need to do to accomplish this and make it your goal.

8. Although sex is important, a rapper's life is crazy! A man will stick with a woman who brings him PEACE! When he gets home, keep it mellow and smooth. Crazy bipolar chicks are destined to remain single!

Coco is a businesswoman, TV personality; a fitness, swimsuit, and *Playboy* model; and has been happily married to rapper Ice-T for many years. She has appeared on more than fifty magazine covers and has her own clothing line coming out. You can find her on the web at CocosWorld.com or watch her on *Ice Loves Coco* on the E! Network.

10 VERY DEEP THOUGHTS ON SEX AND LOVE

1. David Lee Roth
"It's not who wants to sleep with you; it's who wants to sleep with you again."

2. Bret Michaels
"I found out that the more open you are, the more fun you have—having fun immediately turns girls on. I've also realized that self-deprecation…I watch some of my buddies bomb miserably. They would go to be at a club and we'd be hanging out. Girls like to go out, they like to party, what they don't like is for you to pick them up and tell them how much you make." (Sirius Radio, Feb. 4, 2009)

3. Madonna
"Women are here to smash man's ego, plain and simple. Accept this and life will be better…. [A]lso, women like it when men tell them they look nice. If you want more than that you will have to pay for it." (*That's What SHE Said: Women Reveal What Men Really Need to Know*)

4. Keith Richards

"I have never put the make on a girl in my life. I just don't know how to do it. My instincts are always to leave it to the woman." (*Life*)

5. Pete Wentz

"You can definitely tell who's interested in you and who's platonic by paying attention to how a guy moves around you. When I was in high school, my thing was to get as close as humanly possible to a girl and just make her have to kiss me! You do the hug that's too close, where your mouth is close to hers and you kinda feel it out a little bit." (*Seventeen*)

6. Snoop Dogg

The Dogg says that the most important relationship skill is "communication, and being able to fight and get back up. To have misunderstanding and get some understanding." (*People*, June 9, 2008)

7. Rod Stewart

"It's such a rarity for people to stay together that 68 percent of marriages fail. I don't want to urinate on the party, but one must consider that before getting married. The vows should be written like a dog's license that has to be renewed every year." (*Daily Mail*, Jan. 31, 2010)

8. Lady Gaga

"If you can't get to know them, you shouldn't have sex with them." (E!)

9. Nick Cave

"I think there's some very bracing and sobering lessons that can be learnt from love. It doesn't really go the way it's supposed to go, or the way I've always believed that should be, which is the way we're constantly fed about the idea of love and particularly about committed relationships like marriage. That love, in terms of relationships actually has little to do with things at all…It's about a commitment to a greater thing and that is the relationship and the relationship being the commitment of two people." (*I Magazine*, 1997)

10. Reverend Run

"You just have to be able to compromise with your wife as far as I'm concerned. If she has a deep desire to do something you may want to give in to that. My motto is 'Happy wife, happy life.'" (BET.com)

SEAN YSEULT'S TOP 7 SEXIEST SPOTS IN NEW ORLEANS

Sex and drugs and rock 'n' roll—some things just go good together. Sure, there's plenty of all three of these in New Orleans, but we have two other members in this debaucherous club as well: cocktails and food. If you've ever been to New Orleans, you will know that our food is more decadent than sex itself. And our cocktails? Fancy or down and dirty, cheap, heavy on the pour, and round the clock, twenty-four hours. Most hookups happen in bars, but in New Orleans there are plenty of glamorous restaurants (with full bars of course) where the alcohol and flirting flow freely. The following seven spots were picked for their perfect combinations of décor, ambience, music, cocktails, food, and of course, their great crowds.

1. Bouligny Tavern
This is the newest hot spot in New Orleans, and at the very top of my list. Maybe it's the dark golden lighting emanating out of exposed '70s bulbs, dangling down from the brown leather or smoky glass ceiling tiles. Or maybe it's the feeling that you entered a back room at the Playboy Club circa 1972. Besides the décor, there's also great music. The DJs spin rare vinyl at all times, including lovely exotica and other music that really keeps things flowing. The last time I was in here I saw Reggie Bush on the couch, surrounded by beautiful people including chicks hotter than his ex, Kim Kardashian. Sorry, rockers, but in New Orleans there's nothing that gets locals more worked up than being in the same room with a Saint! *(3641 Magazine Street, 504-891-1810)*

2. Patois
Way uptown and tucked away in a neighborhood filled with beautiful nineteenth-century estates, this dark, cozy restaurant brings New Orleans sexy to the table—and the bar. Everyone is dressed up, the bar has top-notch booze, and the bartenders are friendly neighborhood folk, heavy on the pour. This place makes *the* best mint julep I have ever had, hands down. If the owner's not sharing shots of whiskey with you, you might be enjoying indulgent local cuisine at its best: gulf shrimp and chorizo over Manchego spoon bread, crispy pork belly and seared scallops with a cane syrup and spicy mustard drizzle—chef Aaron Burgau knows decadence. *(6078 Laurel Street, 504-895-9441)*

3. The Delachaise

This freestanding, beautiful old train car happens to also be a bar with gorgeous lighting, good-looking people, and tasty delicacies inside. Why do I keep mentioning food? Because it's integral to our city. New Orleanians are a lot like Europeans—we know if you are going to keep drinking until the sun comes up, it's important to have a bite of something now and then. You're in good hands at the Delachaise, which offers everything from cheese plates to steak frites. Sometimes the crowd can get über-hip or über-collegiate; there's no way to tell until you get there. But it *will* get very crowded late at night. *(3442 St. Charles Avenue, 504-895-0858)*

4. La Crepe Nanou

The most romantic restaurant in New Orleans. The lighting, décor, and food make you feel as though you have stumbled upon the best-kept secret in a small village in France. Because they don't take reservations, there are always a number of people sipping wine at the bar, in the street (it's legal here, ya know), checking each other out, and anticipating their evening. With French comfort food to be shared, like mussels and frites, fondue, steaks, French onion soup, and great affordable bottles of French wine, this is a fantastic place for a date. Just off of Prytania Street, this is an uptown hangout where people dress up and look good—even the staff is easy on the eye. Never lacking in ambience, this is the place to start your evening. *(1410 Robert Street, 504-899-2670)*

5. One Eyed Jacks

If you've ever dreamt of coming to New Orleans, you're probably picturing spending your evenings in a place like this. Dripping in decadence and grandeur, the club looks like a brothel from the 1800s. Being in the heart of the French Quarter, who knows? This building probably was a brothel at one point! Ornate Victorian wallpaper, huge antique mirrors and chandeliers, leather banquettes and booths give the vibe. Hot bartenders and a crowd of locals, visitors, and celebrities all mix up to fill this nightclub and add to the excitement. Whenever famous actors are in town filming, they always end up spending their evening here. And when great bands are in town, they're either playing on the velvet-draped stage or hanging out after their gig at the arena. It always adds a little excitement to a club when you run into Robert Plant, or see Jude Law there six nights in a row. *(615 Toulouse Street, 504-569-8361)*

6. Mimi's in the Marigny

Hopping over to the Marigny, Mimi's has it all—great ambience, great wine, tapas, drinks at great prices, and great entertainment. There is an amazing upstairs space to hang out on couches and watch live music, or sneak off onto one of the secluded balconies. Many nights I have gone there for drinks and to see what locals are out, only to be pleasantly surprised by free local music such as the Hot Club of New Orleans. (Hint: Make sure to tip well, it's common courtesy here. Just because the music or your drink was cheap doesn't mean you should be!) They also have DJ nights upstairs, which can get rowdy. *(2601 Royal Street, 504-942-0690)*

7. Bacchanal

Cut over to the Bywater to see what the buzz is on this place. Many seek it out now as the hip place they saw on HBO's *Treme*, but it is still packed with locals looking to enjoy wine, cheap gourmet eats, and free live music. It is also enough off of the beaten path that it will never become too touristy. Although I love the cavernous front room, filled with wine bottles and featuring low lighting and a cat or two, the courtyard is the hot spot. It is truly gorgeous, and typical of New Orleans outdoor culture. Many buildings have lovely balconies and hidden courtyards, to take advantage of the mild weather, but as a visitor you rarely get to experience these private realms. This courtyard is lit up with torches as the sun goes down, adding to the ambience. Sunday night is really *the* night, but it seems lately they have something going on almost every night. *(600 Poland Avenue, 504-948-9111)*

Sean Yseult was the bassist in White Zombie and now plays with Rock City Morgue, outta New Orleans. She recently wrote a book about her experiences called *I'm in the Band: Notes from the Chick in White Zombie.* Find out more at SeanYseult.com.

12 THINGS SID LOVED ABOUT NANCY

Sid Vicious and Nancy Spungeon's impact on rock 'n' roll romance cannot be underestimated. He was the doomed bassist of the Sex Pistols, she was the lunatic blond junkie from Pennsylvania. Blessed with an iconic look and absolutely zero in the way of bass-playing ability, Sid was said by some to have been a virgin when he met Nancy. This handwritten list is kept in the Hard Rock's collection of rock memorabilia and is titled "What Makes Nancy So Great by Sidney."

1. Beautiful
2. Sexy
3. Beautiful figure
4. Great sense of humour
5. Makes extremely interesting conversation
6. Witty
7. Has beautiful eyes
8. Has fab taste in clothes
9. Has the most beautiful wet pussy in the world
10. Even has sexy feet
11. Is extremely smart
12. A great Hustler

4 RIDICULOUSLY RETRO RELATIONSHIP GEMS FROM ROCK STAR WIVES

1. Sharon Osbourne

"If [your] husband isn't getting a blow job when he's on tour in Canada and you're in bloody England, he's either gay or a mutant. As long as he doesn't know her name, doesn't get her phone number, and doesn't do it a second time, it's okay." (*Blender*, Dec. 2004)

2. Tawny Kitaen (David "Whitesnake" Coverdale's ex)

"Look, the way you get these guys is, you don't sleep with them. The girls that give it up quickly are called groupies." (*Blender*, Dec. 2005)

3. Etty Lau Farrell (Perry Farrell's wife)

"Having just come off the road, he's got a tour manager, he's got a production manager, all he has to do is get up and brush his teeth. So when he comes back from the road he's still kind of living that life a little bit. I think all men like to be taken care of." (*Married to Rock*, E! Network)

4. Iman (supermodel, TV presenter, entrepreneur, Mrs. David Bowie)

"I vowed to myself when I got married that I would cook every night. I find it very therapeutic." (*Harper's Bazaar*, Nov. 9, 2010)

MUSIC'S TOP 10 SHORTEST MARRIAGES

Something like 50 percent of all marriages end in divorce anyway, but when you add fame, drugs, booze, and groupies into the mix, that percentage seems to nearly double. Here are some of rock's most fleeting unions.

I. Britney Spears and Jason Alexander

Duration: 55 hours

One can only imagine why these two nitwits married in Vegas, but within 55 hours, the pop star's lawyers made the whole thing go bye-bye. When asked about his brief time as Mr. Britney Spears, the groom told *Access Hollywood*, "It was just crazy, man!"

2. Dennis Hopper and Michelle Phillips

Duration: Eight days

When you wake up the morning after your wedding so wasted that you don't recognize your bride, that's clue number one that you're probably not husband material. Subsequently handcuffing your new bride so she can't run away (not because you're into that kind of thing) would be the number two indicator.

3. Lisa Marie Presley and Nicolas Cage

Duration: Three months

It's no secret that Cage has been obsessed with the King since he came into the public eye. When he nabbed Elvis's daughter, he must've thought he hit the jackpot. Unfortch, Lisa Marie thought different and filed for divorce about ninety days after sealing the deal; releasing a press release that said, "I'm sad about this, but we shouldn't have been married in the first place. It was a big mistake."

4. Lisa Marie Presley and Michael Jackson

Duration: Two years

You'll notice a couple of repeat offenders on this list and Lisa Marie is one of them. Though her marriage to the late King of Pop lasted two years, much of that time was spent apart. And even though she assured Oprah that theirs was a love (gag) match, the extreme lack of chemistry during their public kiss on the MTV Awards still raises eyebrows.

5. Pam Anderson and Kid Rock

Duration: Four months

When PBR poster children Pam Anderson and Kid Rock can't keep it together, what hope do the rest of the folks down the trailer park have?

6. Kenny Chesney and Renée Zellweger

Duration: Four months

When the emaciated actress filed for an annulment just a few months after marrying the country singer, she said their parting was on account of "fraud." While there've been rumors about Mr. Chesney's sexuality, nobody's ever cleared up just what he'd been fibbing about.

7. Jennifer Lopez and Ojani Noa

Duration: Eleven months

J.Lo met Noa when he was a waiter and she was on her way up. They divorced less than a year after marrying, but she hired him to manage a restaurant after he signed a confidentiality agreement. Since then Noa has attempted to publish a book about their relationship and release what some are saying is a sex tape. Lopez's lawyers squashed him like a bug.

8. Jennifer Lopez and Chris Judd

Duration: One year, one month

When Jenny from the Block married choreographer Chris Judd, it was her second marriage, his first. Alas, their torrid tango only lasted a little over a year. Who knows— maybe by the time this book is published, she'll be done with Marc Anthony too. Stop the presses: yup!

9. Amy Winehouse and Blake Fielder Civil

Duration: Two years

The only thing shocking about their divorce is that it took so long (two years) and that *he* was the one who filed the papers. After Fielder-Civil completed his sentenced stints in prison and rehab, the two were set to remarry, when news of a child he'd fathered while still married to Amy hit the fan. Oopsy.

IO. Fred Durst and Esther Nazarov
Duration: 42 days
Looks-challenged Limp Bizkit front man Durst proved his own personal bizkit wasn't so flaccid when he released a puke-inducing sex tape in 2005. And yet somehow, even with his naked can making the rounds on the Internet, he managed to convince some broad to walk down the aisle with him. Luckily for her, she sobered up a little over a month later and the two filed for divorce pronto.

HONORABLE MENTION

Paul McCartney and Heather Mills
Though the pair put in a respectable four years together (for which Ms. Mills was awarded something like 25 million pounds), they deserve mention for the sheer acrimony of their divorce. Mills complained that McCartney was a "boring old fart" and later threatened to release taped sessions he'd had with his therapist. McCartney reportedly called the marriage one of the biggest mistakes of his life.

5 MOST HEINOUS ROCK SPOUSES

You're probably thinking that Yoko Ono will be at the top of the list, but you're wrong. The quirky Japanese songstress has long been blamed for breaking up the Beatles and ruining John Lennon's life, but the truth is, the Beatles had run their course and John Lennon was, by many accounts, a physically abusive, philandering jerk of a spouse. Here are some partners you *really* wouldn't want to say "I do" to.

I. Blake Fielder-Civil
Some husbands give their new brides a ring or some other token of their affection. Blake "Incarcerated" showed Amy Winehouse how to shoot smack, smoke crack, and cut herself. Now granted, while nobody forced Amy to become the mess she quickly became, Fielder-Civil is the definition of "bad influence." If you have any doubts, just look at her before and after photos.

2. Courtney Love

Even if she didn't arrange to have Kurt Cobain murdered (as many believe), Courtney Love wasn't exactly a loving, wonderful wife. According to an infamous story in *Vanity Fair*, which she later denied, Love claimed to have shot heroin throughout her pregnancy with daughter Frances Bean Cobain. She and Cobain were reportedly on the verge of divorce when he turned up dead. Since his death, she's pissed off every member of Nirvana, has been arrested for drugs countless times, and recently beat out Dina Lohan and Whitney Houston and Bobby Brown when she was named the eighth-worst celebrity parent by *Fox News*.

3. Ike Turner

Married anywhere between five and thirteen times, Ike Turner is best known for beating the crap out of Tina Turner. Anyone who watched Angela Bassett channel Ms. Turner in *What's Love Got to Do with It* was left with a deep hatred for that nasty old coot. Though Ike denied beating Tina, in his 2001 biography, *Taking Back My Name*, he clarified, "Sure, I've slapped Tina…. There have been times when I punched her to the ground without thinking. But I have never beat her."

4. Sid Vicious and Nancy Spungeon

Because Sid allegedly murdered Nancy, he's obviously going to come out on top as the greater of two evils, but Nancy was reportedly just as big a nightmare as her drug-addled beau. In fact, before Nancy introduced him to heroin, Sid was a bit of a babe in the woods, only dabbling in shooting speed with his mom (who later supplied him with the dope that killed him).

5. Phil Spector

Even before he was stripped of his wig and sent off to the pokey for murder, Phil Spector was not exactly a sweetheart. Ronnie Spector of the Ronettes had the misfortune of marrying Phil, who immediately imprisoned her in their home, threatening her with attack dogs and guns if she tried to leave. If that wasn't terrifying enough, he showed her a glass-topped gold coffin that he promised to display her body in if she were ever silly enough to make an attempt. Lucky for her she did manage to escape before his violence escalated to murder.

28 INSTANCES OF HOT ROCK PROGENY

If he's successful enough, even the most trollish rock star can nab a model bride (or baby mama), which is why nine out of ten rock sprogs are incredibly good looking. Here are some of the finest, listed by parentage.

1. Keith Richards + Patti Hansen = Theodora and Alexandra Richards
2. Steven Tyler + Bebe Buell = Liv Tyler
2a. Steven Tyler + Cyrinda Foxe = Mia Tyler
2b. Steven Tyler + Teresa Barrick = Chelsea Tallarico
3. Pearl Lowe + Gavin Rossdale = Daisy Lowe
4. Nick Cave + Beau Lazenby = Jethro Lazenby (Cave)
5. Kate McGarrigle + Loudon Wainwright III = Rufus and Martha Wainwright
6. Tim Buckley + Mary Guibert = Jeff Buckley
7. Bob Dylan + Sara Lownds = Jakob Dylan
8. Alice Cooper + Sheryl Goddard = Calico Cooper
9. Ravi Shankar + Sue Jones = Norah Jones
10. Paul Weller + Dee C. Lee = Leah Weller
11. Mick Jagger + Marsha Hunt = Karis Jagger
11a. Mick Jagger + Bianca Jagger = Jade Jagger
11b. Mick Jagger + Jerry Hall = Elizabeth, James, Georgie, and Gabriel
12. Joe Walsh + Juanita Boyer = Lucy Walsh
13. Simon Le Bon + Yasmin Parvaneh = Amber, Saffron and Tallulah
14. Phil Collins + Jill Tavelman = Lily Collins
15. Donna Summers + Bruce Sudano = Brooklyn Sudano
16. Lenny Kravitz + Lisa Bonet = Zoe Kravitz
17. John Phillips + Michelle Phillips = Chynna Phillips
17a. John Phillips + Geneviève Waïte = Bijou Phillips
18. Elvis Presley + Priscilla Ann Wagner = Lisa Marie Presley
19. Lisa Marie Presley + Danny Keough = Riley Keough
20. Kurt Cobain + Courtney Love = Frances Bean Cobain
21. Marvin Gaye + Janis Hunter = Nona Gaye
22. Donovan + Enid Karl = Ione Skye and Donovan Leitch
23. Grace Slick + Paul Kantner = China Kantner
24. Frank Zappa + Adelaide Gail Sloatman = Moon Unit, Dweezil, Ahmet, and Diva Zappa
25. Madonna + Carlos Leon = Lourdes Leon

26. Stephen Stills + Véronique Sanson = Chris Stills
27. Gene Simmons + Shannon Tweed = Nick and Sophie Simmons
28. Kim Gordon + Thurston Moore = Coco Gordon-Moore

THE 10 WORST PARENTS IN ROCK

I. Anne Beverley

Sid Vicious's mom wasn't exactly June Cleaver. Instead of bringing her only son
cookies and milk, Sid's old pal Jah Wobble reports, "I recall seeing him use a syringe
to inject drugs with his mum. I was sixteen; it was a shocking and stark image to
behold. To me, at that age, your mum was someone who left your tea in the oven,
not someone who you banged up drugs with." Beverley kicked Vicious out of the
house when he was sixteen, allegedly telling him, "It's either you or me, and it's not
going to be me. I have got to try to preserve myself and you just fuck off." The two
later reconciled and as a symbol of her love, Mommy stuffed her snatch with dope
and smuggled it into prison for him.

2. John Phillips

Shooting drugs with your kid is one thing, but John Phillips took it several steps
further. When Mackenzie Phillips was only ten, he taught her how to roll joints.
By the time she was seventeen, he had her banging coke. A year later, he raped her
while she was unconscious after a drug binge. And so began a ten-year-long sexual
relationship, which Mackenzie has finally stopped labeling "consensual."

3. Murry Wilson, father of Beach Boys Dennis, Carl, and Brian

Murry Wilson was one sick fuck. The drunken Wilson dad was extremely violent
with his kids, scaring them by removing his glass eye when they were young and
then progressing onto beatings as they got older. He beat Brian so brutally with a
two-by four it caused permanent deafness in his right ear. The most notorious of
Murry's punishments was when he forced Brian to defecate onto a piece of paper
that he then showed the rest of the family. No wonder that when Murry pulled the
croak in 1973, Brian and Dennis were AWOL from the funeral.

4. Joe Jackson

Freak shows like La Toya and, most famously, Michael Jackson aren't just born, they're created. And whether it's owing to drugs or booze or because he's just plain crazy, Jackson family patriarch Joe Jackson is one creepy motherfucker. Marlon Jackson recalls one instance when Joseph, who brutally beat his cash-cow brood whenever they missed a note, held young Michael upside down by one leg and "pummeled him over and over again with his hand, hitting him on his back and buttocks." When Michael died he made sure that his father was left out of his will, which may explain Joseph's bizarre self-promotion efforts at the BET Awards honoring Michael, just three days after the singer's death. Or not.

5. Michael Jackson

He dressed his kids like sideshow performers, dangled them from hotel windows, and gave them the crappest collection of names ever. And while none of them bear even a passing resemblance to him, at least Jackson left them well off when he died. Which is a good thing, because they're going to have some serious therapy bills.

6. Courtney Love and Kurt Cobain

They shot heroin while she was pregnant with Frances and then bragged about it to a *Vanity Fair* reporter (whom they later sued for libel). The two apparently continued to do drugs nonstop until Kurt finally killed himself when his daughter, Frances, was only a year and a half old. Over the years Courtney has slipped in and out of lucidity, bashed a fan on the head with a mic stand, starved herself to fit into couture, and basically continued to be a living, breathing embodiment of bat-shit cuckoo. In 2009, custody of Frances was transferred to her paternal aunt and grandmother, and shortly thereafter, the sensible then-seventeen-year-old filed a restraining order against her mom.

7. Hank Harrison (Courtney's dad)

But did Courtney ever have a chance of being normal? Her father, Hank, once told a reporter, "Kurt [Cobain] would probably be alive today if he hadn't met her." Courtney says Daddy Dearest fed her LSD when she was only seven and disappeared from her life for years, finally resurfacing to assure the press that his daughter had actually hired someone to kill Cobain. Nice!

8. Franklin Moorer (father of country singers Shelby Lynne and Allison Moorer)

When Shelby was seventeen and Allison was thirteen, their alcoholic father murdered their long-suffering mother and then turned the gun on himself. Allison later sang, "I take a pint of whiskey and crack open its lid / I drink the bottle empty just like my poor daddy did." Happily, the two are still alive and making music.

9. Marvin Gaye Sr.

When singer Marvin Gaye became hopelessly addicted to cocaine in the early '80s, he probably thought moving in with his minister dad would be the right thing to do. Unfortunately, the senior Gaye wasn't very Christ-like and was consumed by jealousy over his son's success. On April 1, 1984, the two had an argument that ended when Mr. Gaye Sr. shot and murdered his son.

10. Pete Doherty

The surprise here isn't that Pete Doperty is a bad dad—the shocking thing is that someone willingly not only had sex with the pustule-peppered rocker, but chose to have a child with him. Actually, *two* different women did so, though Pete only sees one of his sons. As for the other, Pete told a reporter, "Poor little fu@&*er. My sister sees him all the time, so there's affection as a family for him."

THE 12 LONGEST MARRIAGES IN ROCK

When Pam Anderson ditches Kid Rock after a couple months, pretty much anything over a year constitutes an LTR in the music world. After all, rock stars are faced with temptation every single second of every day—whether in the form of groupies, gold diggers, or pliant fans. Expecting a guy who sells out stadiums every night to remain faithful is a fool's game. Here are some marriages that managed to last in spite of all the temptations and trials.*

1. Bono and Ali Hewson

The fact that Ali has her own clothing line and a bunch of kids to take care of means she's not sitting around on her ass, waiting for her man to get home from touring. And it seems to be working, as they've been together for more than twenty-five years.

2. Bruce Springsteen and Patti Scialfa

Springsteen followed the opposite trajectory of most rock stars, dumping the much younger model he married for the age-appropriate average-looking guitarist in his band. Married since 1991, the two appear to have a solid union and three children.

3. David Bowie and Iman

When the news broke that Bowie was marrying Iman, I'm sure many people heard that as "a man," due to the singer's well-publicized bisexuality. But the striking Somalian supermodel and the Thin White Duke have been together since 1992. The two have one child together (imagine that cheekbones on that kid!) and one stepchild apiece. As Bowie once put it, "Turns out I was a closet heterosexual."

4. Jon and Dorothea Bon Jovi

It hasn't always been a smooth road for the mop-topped rocker and his high school sweetheart. There was the time he dumped her for Diane Lane, only to dump *her* when she got too close to Richie Sambora, which sent him running back to Dorothea, whom he married in Vegas in 1989. Jon admits, "I've not been a saint. I've had my lapses." Despite those lapses, the couple have four kids together and seem to have a low-key happy marriage.

5. Sting and Trudie Styler

Together for nearly thirty years, these two put the ay-yi-yi in TMI with all their blathering on about their tantric sex practices. Sting told one journalist, "My church happens to be the person I live with. She is my connection to the sacred." Their sacred sex seems to be working, because they show no signs of splitting up anytime soon.

6. Pat Benatar and Neil "Spyder" Giraldo

The couple met when Chrysalis hired Neil to be the lead guitarist on Benatar's breakout album, *In the Heat of the Night*, and married in 1982. They have two children together and still tour occasionally.

7. Ozzy and Sharon Osbourne

Anyone who's seen an episode of *The Osbournes* knows who wears the pants in this family, and maybe that's the reason that the Osbournes have one of the few marriages that has stood not only the test of time (they have been married since '82), but also the ravages of the reality television.

8. Keith Richards and Patti Hansen

Another model/rock star pairing, these two have been officially together since 1983, marrying that year on Keith's fortieth birthday. Perhaps part of the reason for their relationship's success, Keith told the *Daily Mail*, "When I'm at home I do as I'm told: 'Yes, darling, no, darling,' like any other guy."

9. Paul and Linda McCartney

Paul and Linda were married for just under thirty years when Linda succumbed to breast cancer. The couple played music together, were vegetarian activists, and produced three kids—one of whom is the fashion designer Stella McCartney.

10. John Lydon and Nora Forster

When the punk rock icon married the fourteen-years-older publishing heiress (who was also the late Slit Ari Up's mom), it was rumored he'd done it for a stake in her fortune. Nearly thirty years later, he shrugs off the naysayers, insisting, "I know I didn't marry Nora for her money. I'm committed to Nora and, in my eyes, when you make a commitment you stick to it. I'm lucky—I don't need a sham Hollywood marriage."

11. John Lennon and Yoko Ono

Though they were on-again/off-again for a few years there, John and Yoko were married in 1969 and stayed that way until his murder in 1980. During their honeymoon the pair created a set of lithographs commemorating their romantic vacation. They must've had a damn good dirty time because eight of the fourteen were judged to be obscene and were confiscated. Fairly or not, Ono is often credited as being the impetus for the Beatles' breakup and for that she gets a big ol' high five.

12. Charlie Watts and Ann Shepherd

Married since *1964* (!!!!!) Watts and Shepherd currently hold the record for the longest marriage in rock 'n' roll. Known for being the gentleman of the band, Watts does confess to a three-year dalliance with drugs and alcohol, though he's notorious for turning down groupies' advances.

---

* There's no guarantee that any of these couples will be together by the time this book goes into print, but even if they've split, they've still all had a good long run.

4 TAKES ON INFIDELITY

1. Jerry Hall: Take it from one who should know

"There is no way a woman would ever leave her family for a teenager like [Ron Wood did]. No. It's about a fear of dying for men: They want to stay immortal. But you know what, honey? We're all dying every day—it's just that women are more deeply rooted in reality." (*Telegraph*, Oct. 27, 2009)

2. Valerie Bertinelli: The girl next door wasn't so squeaky clean

"I wasn't an angel, either. I cheated, too. He claims to this day that I cheated first, but I don't know. I don't know about the timing." (*The Oprah Winfrey Show*, June 23, 2008)

3. Seal is no fool

"I met Heidi when I was forty and I'd done all the messing around. In fact, I've probably done enough for four lifetimes. I was no saint. But there comes a point where you're either going to grow up or you're going to be some old rock star wanker who can't keep it in his pants, an embarrassment to his kids. And that's nothing to do with Heidi…it's just not me." (*Mirror*, Sept. 19, 2010)

4. Dolly Parton and Carl Dean go with don't ask, don't tell

"I don't want to know it, if he's cheating on me. If I'm cheating on him, he wouldn't want to know it—and if we do, if that's what's making it work, then that's fine, too." (*Woman's Day*, Dec. 6, 2007)

19 SONGS ABOUT CHEATING (AND BEING CHEATED ON)

1. "Not Big," Lily Allen

Lily proves she's going to take her man's cheating lying down with this stellar line, "Let's see how you feel in a couple of weeks, when I work my way through your mates."

2. "Another Girl," the Beatles

Paul was a cheater...

3. "Norwegian Wood (This Bird Has Flown)," the Beatles

...and so was John.

4. "High Fidelity," Elvis Costello

Elvis's wandering willy was documented in Bebe Buell's memoir and according to academics at the University of Chicago, this song "exploits the multiple meanings of fidelity by linking unfaithful romantic liaisons and the distorted transmission of sound."

5. "I Want You," Bob Dylan

This song is allegedly about the woman with the magical vagina, Anita Pallenberg, with whom Dylan was dallying while she was still with Brian Jones.

6. "Lyin' Eyes," the Eagles

You can't hide 'em.

7. "Who's That Girl?" the Eurythmics

You know what happens when you step out on the woman you're in a band with? She writes a song about your cheating ass, that's what.

8. "Savin' All My Love for You," Whitney Houston

Years before she was asking Bobby Brown to reach up her rectum and dig a dookie out, Whitney had this hit about being the other woman.

9. and 10. "You Ain't Woman Enough" and "Family Tree," Loretta Lynn

Cheating is a common theme in country music and Loretta Lynn has a bunch of songs about it. These two—both addressing the ho-bags who stole her man—were written nearly thirty years apart (1966 and 2004, respectively), and make it clear that Loretta should've been less concerned about confronting the other lady and more concerned with kicking her philandering man's ass.

11. "Jolene," Dolly Parton

Dolly's heartbreaking plea to the would-be other woman was based on a flirty bank teller. Parton told NPR, "She got this terrible crush on my husband, and he just loved going to the bank because she paid him so much attention. It was kinda like a running joke between us—when I was saying, 'Hell, you're spending a lot of time at the bank. I don't believe we've got that kind of money.'"

12. "O.P.P.," Naughty by Nature

Is it "other people's property?" Or "other people's pussy/penis?"

13. "If That's Your Boyfriend (He Wasn't Last Night), Meshell Ndegeocello

Do you really wanna get in the middle of this catfight? "You can say I'm wrong, say I ain't right, But if that's your boyfriend he wasn't last night." Burn!

14. "Me and Mrs. Jones," Billy Paul

This one-hit wonder and Mrs. Jones—they got a thing goin' on. Even though they both know that it's wrong.

15. "Confessions Pt. 2," Usher

Part one apparently involved admitting to sticking it elsewhere. The sequel involves a bun in the other broad's oven. Tsk, tsk, Usher. Is this why your marriage lasted like five seconds?

16. "Guilty," Barbra Streisand and Barry Gibb

The real guilt should stem from unleashing this inexplicable hit upon the listening public.

17. "Smell Yo Dick," Riskay

Suspect your man's cheating? You could have him followed, or hack into his phone or e-mail. Then again, you could just have him drop trou and nuzzle his nutsack like Riskay does in this song.

18. "My Affair," Kirsty MacColl

This song is based on that old chestnut, the revenge fuck. Wherein your husband's been sticking it to anything with a pulse and then has the nerve to get cranky when you start doing the same. "Now it's no concern of yours if I sleep with the president!"

19. "Sleepin' with My Fonk," Sir Mix-a-Lot

Sticking with the revenge theme, Sir Mix is seen driving off with his main rival's girl only to discover his rival then scooped up Mix's lady for some lovin'. Relationships are complicated!

4 BANDS THAT SURVIVED ROMANTIC BREAKUPS

I. No Doubt
When Tony Kanal dumped Gwen Stefani, she was heartbroken, but the resulting musical output propelled them to huge success. Her loss was the band's gain.

2. Fleetwood Mac
Fleetwood Mac are the *Peyton Place* of the music industry. Christine McVie joined the band after marrying John McVie. Lindsey Buckingham and his then-girlfriend Stevie Nicks joined and they achieved megasuccess in 1975, just as original member Mick Fleetwood's marriage was imploding. John and Christine's divorce followed soon after and Buckingham and Nicks also broke up. The band eventually split for twenty years, but got over their acrimony to reunite and cash in.

3. White Stripes
When fame hit, Jack and Meg White started the rumor they were brother and sister, though it was quickly discovered they'd been married and then divorced in 2000. They must've had the most amicable split in the history of the world, because they stayed together—both remarrying others—until 2011.

4. Jefferson Airplane
Grace Slick's first interband relationship was with drummer Spencer Dryden. After that ended, she moved in with guitarist Paul Kantner. The two had a child in 1971, though Grace left Kantner for a J.A. roadie. Despite all the dramz, the band stayed together. (Though whether they should have bothered is up for debate.)

PART TWO: DRUGS

THE PRACTICAL DRUG USER

KEITH RICHARDS'S 12-STEP GUIDE TO HOW THE VERY WEALTHY, WORLD-TRAVELING, SUPERSTAR JUNKIE GETS HIS FIX IN NEW YORK CITY

1. Call your dealer ahead of time—from London—and arrange for him to meet you at the Plaza Hotel.

2. Make certain you're wearing a smart hat (though if you're a woman, a corsage would work) and use the needle from a fresh hypodermic to affix feather to natty hatband.

3. Get high before boarding; double-check you haven't forgotten a lump of hash or stray roach in any of your pockets.

4. Pass through customs ignoring the agent's side-eye and cheerfully sign autographs for adoring fans.

5. Check into hotel, meet dealer, and complete cash transaction. Not necessarily in that order.

6. Order exactly one overpriced cup of room-service coffee. Dump the coffee down the toilet, trash the milk and sugar, leave the cup and saucer outside your door. The only reason you ordered a twelve-buck cuppa joe was for the teaspoon you'll need for cooking.

7. Realize that while you have the needle, you don't have a barrel to hold the dope.

8. Discover that the Plaza Hotel is across the street from the world's greatest toy store, FAO Schwarz.

9. Dodge fans, get a cart and start filling it with teddy bears, remote-control cars, and other sundry beard-toys as you head to the third floor to get what you came for: a little plastic doctor kit, containing a fake hypodermic needle equipped with a real barrel that fits your needle.

10. Make chirpy small talk at the register with clerk who's equal parts frightened and excited to be selling plush toys to the Great Keith Richards.

11. Casually exit the store and then haul ass back to hotel room to fix.

12. Mission accomplished. Nod happily.

Paraphrased from pp. 404–405 of *Life* (Little Brown).

THE DRUGS DO WORK—8 PEOPLE TELL HOW

1. Maynard James Keenan (Tool)

"I think psychedelics play a major part in what we do, but having said that, I feel that if somebody's going to experiment with those things they really need to educate themselves about them…. The trick is to use the drugs once to get there, and maybe spend the next ten years trying to get back there without the drug." (*Penthouse*, June 2001)

2. "Nice People Take Drugs." (slogan for 2009 British ad campaign for drug policy reform)

3. Paul McCartney

"[LSD] opened my eyes. We only use one-tenth of our brain. Just think of what we could accomplish if we could only tap that hidden part! It would mean a whole new world if politicians would take LSD. There wouldn't be any more war or poverty or famine." (*Queen* magazine)

4. Dave Mustaine (Megadeth)

"But I had to go through that [addiction], and deal with it all, and without it, my life would be totally different. My problems got very bad, but it was all a learning curve." (Contactmusic.com, May 7, 2007)

5. Noel Gallagher (Oasis)

"I look at Chris Martin, who says he has never taken drugs in his life, and I think he is an idiot. Doing drugs is the most beautiful thing about being in a rock band.... Up until 1998 I must have spent £1 million on drugs—then I stopped, because it is bad for your health, brain, life, and for people around you. But while you use them—except for heroin, which kills people and which I have never tried—as you lot [Italians] would say, 'Mamma Mia.'"(*NME*, July 6, 2009)

6. David Bowie

"Meanwhile, Bowie's *Station to Station* derives at least some of its mesmeric, zombie-eyed power from the fact Bowie wrote it—according to legend—while barricaded into an Egyptian mummy–strewn L.A. house, surviving on a diet of cocaine, milk, and peppers, convinced that witches were trying to steal his semen...." (Luke Lewis, *NME*, Oct. 20, 2009)

7. Fat Mike (NOFX)

"Anybody who knows me well knows I do a lot of drugs. Right now, I just came from a record label meeting. When I'm home and I'm working, I'm sober. When I'm on the road, I'm partying; makes sense, right?" (*Broward–Palm Beach New Times*, Jan 27, 2011)

8. Lady Gaga

"[Using drugs] I really figured out the art I wanted to make and was inspired.... Some people find inspiration in dark places. I guess I'm one of them. What always made me different is that if I was doing drugs I was also making music. I wasn't just doing drugs." (*Q Magazine*, Aug. 2010)

MIKE EDISON'S 5 TIPS FOR SUCCESSFULLY BRINGING DRUGS ACROSS INTERNATIONAL BORDERS WHILE ON TOUR

First, I want to make it very clear to any interested parties that may be reading this that I am of the Hunter Thompson School, meaning there are only two things I do not do with drugs: deal them, or bring them across international borders. Because, really, what is the point? Ask Keith Richards—it's always best to call ahead. That being said, I can confess to, a few times back in *L'age D'or de Gunk Punk*, driving the van across Holland, heading for the German border, when someone suddenly remembers a bag of speed or a block of hash and the conundrum begins. The best thing to do, natch, is ingest them— there is no law against coming into a country stoned or wired. But if you can't do that...

1. Never ever put drugs in your shaving kit—first place they look.
2. Never ever put drugs in the guitar cases—second place they look.
3. Never ever put drugs up your ass. I mean you *can,* but then what are you going to do with them? Seriously.
4. Make sure there are no roaches in the ashtray—customs officials are extra hard on stupid people. When they get done laughing, they will beat you.
5. I have always had good luck hiding contraband in cymbal stands, wrapped in foil and duct tape and tucked in with a drumstick. But now that the whole world knows . . .

Former *High Times* publisher Mike Edison is the author of twenty-eight pornographic novels, and the memoir *I Have Fun Everywhere I Go: Savage Tales of Pot, Porn, Punk Rock, Pro Wrestling, Talking Apes, Evil Bosses, Dirty Blues, American Heroes, and the Most Notorious Magazines in the World.* He is also the putative editor of this book.

NO FUN, MY BABE, NO FUN: 8 ROCKERS WHO JUST SAID NO

I. Ted Nugent

"Honest and intelligent people will remember it for what it really was: the Summer of Drugs." (*Wall Street Journal*, July 3, 2007)

2. Little Steven Van Zandt (E Street Band/*Sopranos*/*Little Steven's Underground Garage*)

"Primal Scream could be the biggest band in the world. They're fantastic when they make rock records once every ten years but man, they can't tour because he's a drug addict or whatever he is. I don't have patience for it. I'm like if you wanna be a drug addict go and be a drug addict—don't waste my time." (*Guardian*, Mar. 25, 2009)

3. Rod Stewart

[Offering advice to his daughter's pal, Paris Hilton.] "Give up the drugs. You don't need them. We've all done it but I've never been a druggie person so I've always been against it." (*Hello!*, Sept. 3, 2010)

4. Bruce Springsteen

"I never did any drugs. When I was at that age when it was popular, I wasn't really in a social scene a whole lot…. Plus, I was very concerned with being in control at the time. I was totally involved in what I was doing, and I had no need for anything else or anybody." (*Bruce Springsteen: Two Hearts: The Definitive Biography, 1972–2003*)

5. Frank Zappa

"Drug use is a problem that faces America today in all age brackets. There's all different kinds of drugs; they're used by all different kinds of Americans and the amount of usage is staggering. I think it's a major problem. It's at least as big a problem as alcoholism or religious fanaticism…. When a person is chemically altered, he is saying to the world at large, 'I am no longer responsible for my activities, because I'm stoned.'" (From a 1981 video interview with Pennsylvania State Trooper Charles Ash as part of an antidrug campaign for the Pennsylvania Public School System)

6. Gene Simmons

"It never interested me. I also never eat bugs, but the French do; they eat grasshoppers and frogs' legs. The idea of numbing my senses does not appeal to me—I have never seen someone drunk act cool, nor have I ever had a conversation with someone that is high that makes sense.... Ultimately, I think too highly of myself to be anything but who I am all the time." (Interview with AskMen.com)

7. Ian "Straight Edge" MacKaye (Minor Threat, Fugazi)

"Someone recently asked me, 'Are you still living this straight-edge lifestyle?' It is a reflection of the perversity of this culture that it would be conventional to think that not putting toxins into your body would somehow be a lifestyle, when in fact, that's life." (*Satya*, Nov. 2006)

8. Hayley Williams (Paramore)

"We're not trying to bang chicks—or guys in my case—after the show, and you're not going to see us in the newspaper arrested for snorting cocaine in some bathroom.... I like to know that I'm in control—that's why I don't do drugs or drink. I did drink for a while growing up, until I realized I was doing it to be cool.... I want everything I say or write to come from the heart, not a pill or a pipe." (*Guardian*, Nov. 4, 2010)

HONORABLE MENTION

Joe Strummer was a well-known fan of the herb, yet in an interview with *High Times*, he admitted, "Well, I think it's better not to take any drug at all. My advice would be, 'Don't bother to take any drugs.' But that's what I say, that's not what I've done." (*High Times*, Jan. 2003)

MICHAEL GONZALES'S 7 GREAT DRUGGY HIP-HOP HITS

1. "The P is Free," Boogie Down Productions
Even at the height of basehead zombies roaming the streets of New York City in the cocaine '80s, it was difficult to a resist a song whose lyrics proclaimed, "The pussy is free, 'cause the crack costs money." Beam me up, Scotty.

2. "Kryptonite," Purple Ribbon All-Stars featuring Big Boi
Other than the green rock that knocks Superman on his ass, I hadn't the slightest idea what OutKast member Big Boi was referring to on this jam. Still, that didn't stop me from wanting to try some.

3. "White Lines (Don't Do It)," Grandmaster Melle Mel
Fresh from the breakup of Grandmaster Flash and the Furious Five, rapper Melle Mel created a cocaine anthem dressed up as an antidrug song. Believe me, no one was fooled.

4. "Because I Got High," Afroman
Howard Stern used to play this song to death. I wanted to write about why I liked it so much, but I forgot.

5. "Candy Shop," 50 Cent
Since vegans and other spoilers keep insisting that sugar is addictive, this track is one of my favorite drug songs. Although when 50 Cent raps, "I'll take you to the candy shop, I'll let you lick the lollipop," I don't think he's talking about Hershey's chocolate.

6. "Blue Magic," Jay-Z
Done for his dope comeback, *American Gangster*, which served as an aural companion piece to the film of the same name, "Blue Magic" was an ode to the heroin gangster Frank Lucas sold in Harlem during the 1970s.

7. "Sippin' on Some Syrup," Three 6 Mafia
Only in America can you write a song that popularizes a new drug mixed with codeine and a few years later win an Oscar. Having drunk this shit once, I now know why the south lost that war: They were sleepy.

MICHAEL GONZALES'S 7 GREAT DRUGGY SOUL SELECTIONS

1. "King Heroin," James Brown
Although James Brown was shaking hands with Tricky Dick Nixon in 1972, that didn't stop him from recording this anti-heroin heartbreaker. Sixteen years later, he was arrested for possession of angel dust.

2. "Angel Dust," Gil Scott-Heron
Is it me or is it crazy that one of the dopest antidrug songs was written by a brilliant songwriter who later became a crackhead?

3. "I Get Lifted," George McCrae
Although McCrae's soul hit later became a disco hit under labelmates KC and the Sunshine Band the following year, this version is masterful.

4. "Brown Sugar," D'Angelo
One of the best weed anthems ever made. One can almost smell the smoke rising from the grooves.

5. "Champagne Supernova," Oasis
Say what you may about Oasis, but these mumble-mouthed lads are my favorite blue-eyed soul boys ever. "Where were you while we were getting high" is like something Marvin Gaye might've sung.

6. "Psychedelic Shack," the Temptations
When folks like Arthur Lee, Jimi Hendrix, and Sly Stone gave black folks permission to be hippies, even Motown got with the program. Tie-dye replaced suits, acid replaced weed, but Berry Gordy still got all the money.

7. "Rehab," Amy Winehouse
"No, no, no," squealed the junkie. Another soul Brit who practiced what she preached.

10 BEATLES DRUGS STORIES

Perhaps because they were around during the same time as the unapologetically debauched Rolling Stones, the four mop-tops from Liverpool always seemed kind of sweet and innocent in comparison. The reality was quite different though. As you'll see here, the Fab Four were quite often the Fucked-Up Foursome.

I. Lennon was a lightweight.

I don't think John [Lennon] ever left my house except horizontally. Or definitely propped up. (Keith Richards remarking on John Lennon's inability to keep up with his own prolific and prodigious drug intake in *Life*)

2. Or it could just mean an annoying world full of people wearing tie-dye and gassing on about their third eyes.

After I took [LSD], it opened my eyes. We only use one-tenth of our brain. Just think what we could accomplish if we could only tap that hidden part. It would mean a whole new world. (Paul McCartney, *Life*, June 19, 1967)

3. The Beatles were a lot more interesting before they started taking acid.

"During those early Hamburg years, the boys from Liverpool experimented with drugs and strippers and ran up huge bar tabs that they couldn't afford to pay. Isn't that more rock 'n' roll than what came later: smoking dope, visiting the maharishi, meditating?" (Rebecca Schiller, "Speed, Strippers, and Fights—the Beatles in Hamburg," *NME*, Aug. 19, 2010)

4. Jeez, that poor Yoko gets blamed for everything!

"George says it was *me* who put John on heroin, but that wasn't true. John wouldn't take anything he didn't want to take." (Yoko Ono, quoted in *The Love You Make*)

5. The same guy who did their veneers also dosed them for the first time. Those were the days—my dentist won't even give me painkillers.

"The forty-five-minute trip took hours to make because George couldn't drive any faster than fifteen kilometers an hour. Cynthia sat in the back, sticking her fingers down her throat, trying to throw up the sugar cube. John couldn't stop talking.... Pattie, frightened and claustrophobic in the small car, begged to stop and sit in a quiet open field alongside the road. John kept laughing and repeating, 'But you can't play football now, Pattie.'" (George and John's first acid trip, *The Love You Make*)

6. Why not just use the roadie's colon?

"I was out in New York and I had all this really good grass. We were about to fly to Japan and I knew I wouldn't be able to get anything to smoke over there. This stuff was too good to flush down the toilet, so I thought I'd take it with me." (Paul McCartney to *Uncut*, talking about getting busted with *seven ounces* of pot in his suitcase)

7. George was busted by a shady cop who later got shitcanned for planting evidence.

"They chose Paul's wedding day to come and do a raid on me, and to this day I'm still having difficulty with my visa to America because of this fella. He came out to my house with about eight other policemen, a policewoman, and a police dog, who happened to be called Yogi—because, I suppose, of the Beatle connection with [the] Maharishi. They thought they'd have a bit of fun." (George Harrison, *The Beatles Anthology*, 2002)

8. Lennon really liked his drugs.

"*Help* was where we turned on to pot and we dropped drink, simple as that. I've always needed a drug to survive. The others, too, but I always had more, more pills, more of everything because I'm more crazy probably." (John Lennon, in an interview with Jann Wenner for *Rolling Stone*, Jan. 21 and Feb. 4, 1971)

9. The Ohio Highway Patrol named their dog after Ringo.

"He helped bring in just over $38 million worth of cocaine, about $9.5 million in marijuana, $2.6 million in heroin, and nearly $2.5 million in cash." (Ringo the Drug-Sniffing Dog's eulogy, WTVG-TV, Toledo, OH, June 3, 2010)

10. Ringo was the smartest Beatle.

He told the *New York Times* he drank to excess because "I was just a terrified little bunny out there, you know?" And yet despite appearing at pro–pot legalization rallies and having done stints in rehab, Ringo was the only Beatle who managed to avoid getting on Johnny Law's bad side. Probably why he—and not John, Paul, or George—got a drug-sniffing dog named after him. Good boy!

THE DARK SIDE

4 OFFENDER HALL-OF-FAMERS

1. Flavor Flav has not only been arrested countless times on various drug possession charges, he's also had his driver's license suspended no fewer than forty-three times!

2. The Rolling Stones' first brush with the law happened in 1965 when Brian, Mick, and Bill were nicked for public urination. After that there were countless drug busts, and several assault cases between the group and a girlfriend (Ron Wood), journalists (Richards), photographers (Jagger and Richards), and police officers.

3. Rapper Lil Wayne has been busted in 2006, 2007, and 2008 for various offenses including possession of a weapon, possession of marijuana, possession of huge amounts of prescription meds, failing to show up in court, possession of a weapon, possession of marijuana...What next, Lil Wayne? He also has "Fear God" tattooed across his eyelids, a couple teardrops inked beside his eyes, a fleur-de-lis on his cheek, and "I am music" scrawled in red ink on his forehead.

4. David Crosby is allegedly clean now (after a liver transplant solved the problem of the one he ruined), but has been arrested numerous times for drug possession of (at different times) heroin, cocaine, weed, and codeine. Once he

was arrested again while on out on bail for other cocaine charges. In 1982 and 2004 he was arrested for weed possession and for carrying a loaded pistol. And this is who Melissa Etheridge picked to sperminate her wife?

4 ZOMBIE ROCKERS: THEY ODed AND CAME BACK FROM THE DARK SIDE

The life of a drug addict is fraught with danger. You risk arrest, getting robbed, and overdosing. Sometimes it's possible to snap an OD out of it with an ice cube up the butt or a walk around the block. Other times the user can lapse into a coma (like Kurt Cobain did a few weeks before his death), and then, of course, there's always the possibility of not waking up ever again. These four dudes actually flatlined and somehow came back from the dead.

1. Nikki Sixx (Mötley Crüe)

Nikki's near-fatal overdose has been documented in *The Dirt*, *Heroin Diaries*, and in countless interviews with the Mötley Crüe bassist. But nobody tells the story quite like then–Guns N' Roses drummer Steven Adler, who recounts finding Sixx on the floor in his book, *My Appetite for Destruction: Sex & Drugs & Guns N' Roses*: "I started smashing him in the head, and I can still hear the sick sound it made when my cast slammed into his face. But Nikki wasn't moving. Not even a groan, despite the freezing cold water, the hammer blows and me screaming at the top of my lungs."

2. Mark Linkous (Sparklehorse)

In 1995, Mark Linkous collapsed from an overdose of Valium and antidepressants and lay on the floor of a London hotel bathroom for fourteen hours before being discovered by a maid. On the way to the hospital, Linkous had a freak heart attack and flatlined for two minutes before being brought back to life. Unfortunately, in 2010, Linkous finished the job when he shot himself in the heart.

3. Phil Anselmo (Pantera)

In 1996, Pantera played the Coca-Cola Starplex outside of Dallas. Anselmo came offstage and injected an assload of heroin, and went down. According to a statement he released, "There was no lights, no beautiful music, just nothing. And then after twenty minutes (from what I heard later) my friends slapped me and poured water over my head all basically trying to revive me. The paramedics finally arrived and all I remember is waking up in the back of an ambulance."

4. Nile Rodgers (Chic)

Nile Rodgers had already been through two near-fatal bouts with alcohol-induced pancreatitis when he nearly died in New York. He describes the scenario: "I had done coke and whatever else, and that's what happened. Nothing glamorous, just a typical alcoholic death. They were able to revive me. Because of the amount of coke in my system, though, my heart kept stopping. Finally, after they tried to revive me the seventh or eighth time, they just gave up. The doctor was filling out the death certificate, and my heart just started beating again."

As of this book's writing, Rodgers was sober, but battling an aggressive form of cancer.

15 WHO CROAKED FROM DRUG–RELATED CAUSES AT 27

Pete Doherty must've breathed a huge sigh of relief once his twenty-eighth rolled around because twenty-seven seems to be *the* age to die of drug-related causes. Choking on vomit, overdoing it with the speedballs, or just mixing pills with booze, check out the way these fourteen people checked out.

1. Jimi Hendrix

It's hard to believe that Jimi Hendrix's entire career spanned only three and a half years, but this high-school dropout who couldn't read a note of music was one of the most influential guitarists in rock history. Unfortunately, he was also a prolific drug taker and died after mixing barbiturates with booze and choking on his own vomit in 1970.

2. Brian Jones (Rolling Stones)

Though the circumstances of Brian Jones's death remain murky to this day, he did have a load of pills and booze in his body. Was it suicide? Who knows? Murder? Someone who was at the house supposedly made a deathbed confession, though he died before it could be verified. Most likely the death was an accident, as swimming and being extremely fucked up aren't a very healthy combination.

3. Janis Joplin

In 1963, Janis hitchhiked from Port Arthur, Texas, to hang out with the hippies in San Francisco (where, P.S., she once smashed a bottle of Southern Comfort over Jim Morrison's head when he got on her nerves). Though booze was her preferred drug of choice, Joplin had a longtime, on-and-off relationship with dope, and a bad batch of heroin killed her on October 4, 1970.

4. Jim Morrison

Speaking of the Lizard King, though Morrison didn't technically die of an overdose, years of drinking and drugging caused him to have the heart attack that killed him in 1971.

5. Rudy Lewis (the Drifters)

Lewis's cause of death was never declared, but the singer was a longtime drug addict, so the police attributed his death to an overdose. His buddies claim he was a binge eater and that more likely that he choked to death on food.

6. Kurt Cobain

Cobain had so much heroin in his system at the time of his death that many people have argued he was too fucked up to have pulled the trigger. British filmmaker Nick Broomfield even advanced the theory that Courtney Love was responsible for his death.

7. Kristen Pfaff (Hole)

Speaking of Courtney Love, Hole bassist Pfaff ODed at twenty-seven, soon after the release of the band's second album, ironically titled, *Live Through This*.

8. Ron "Pigpen" McKernan

The Grateful Dead were more known for weed and psychedelics, but Pigpen's drug of choice was alcohol. Years of heavy drinking caused his stomach to finally give up and hemorrhage in 1973.

9. Jeremy Michael Ward (the Mars Volta)

The Mars Volta were an amazing band that never got as popular as they deserved. Ward was the band's "sound technician," and died of a heroin overdose after returning home from a tour opening for the Red Hot Chili Peppers (who've also had their struggles with dope).

10. Dave Alexander (the Stooges)

Can you imagine how fucked up you must have been to get booted from the Stooges? Drunk Dave Alexander was *that* much of a mess and sadly died from alcohol-related causes.

11. Alan "Blind Owl" Wilson (Canned Heat)

The lead singer/songwriter got his nickname because of his legendary poor eyesight. Wilson was a well-respected bluesman who also seems to have suffered from depression. He had tried to commit suicide twice before he died of a drug overdose in 1970. It's unclear whether his final OD was a suicide or not, because he left no note.

12. Bryan Ottoson (American Head Charge)

The members of this industrial metal band were so drug-addled that their record label let them out of their contract without any penalty. They were on tour with Mudvayne and Life of Agony when guitarist Ottoson was found dead in his bunk. The cause of death: prescription drug overdose.

13. Sean Patrick McCabe (Ink and Dagger)

McCabe was the vocalist for Philadelphia-based punk band Ink and Dagger. He died, asphyxiating on his own vomit, in an Indiana motel room, just after the band had finished recording their final album.

14. Gary Thain (Uriah Heep)

Thain was Uriah Heep's third bassist, but was badly shocked onstage in 1974 and had to leave the band for health-related reasons soon after. By the following year he was dead of a heroin overdose.

15. Amy Winehouse

During the editing of this book, we got the sad news that Amy Winehouse had become the newest member of "The 27 Club."

(VERY) HONORABLE MENTIONS

Bluesmaster Robert Johnson also died at age 27, though his exact cause of death is not known. It's rumored that he died after taking a swig of strychnine-laced whiskey, but some also claim it was syphilis that took his life.

Jean-Michel Basquiat wasn't a rock star, but his work was an integral part of an extremely vibrant, musical time in New York City downtown nightlife and graffiti culture. Unfortunately, an errant speedball killed him in 1988.

11 NOTORIOUS DRUG BUSTS

I. Sister Sinéad calls the coppers on Shane MacGowan
It's one thing to borrow £600 from your pal who is currently going through her nun stage, as O'Connor (née Sister Mary Bernadette) was. It's quite another to march out with the borrowed dough, spend it all on drugs, and begin shooting up right in front of her. O'Connor warned her dentally challenged friend that if he didn't stop it, she'd call the police. He didn't; she did.

2. Doherty earns the nickname "Doperty"
Now Pete Doherty has been arrested more times than anyone can keep track of, but his best happened a few days before Christmas 2009. Not only was he forty minutes late for his court date, but while he was standing (swaying?) before the judge, thirteen wraps of heroin tumbled out of his pocket and onto the courtroom floor. The judge, who fined him £750, was suspicious that anyone could be *that* much of a nitwit. "Either this was sheer stupidity or a ploy to get more publicity," said District Judge Joti Bopa Rai.

3. Isn't this what roadies are for?
In 1980 Paul McCartney and his band Wings flew to Asia for a Japanese tour. On his way through customs he was nabbed with over seven ounces of marijuana in his bags. Not jammed up his ass—tucked away in his suitcase. Sigh. If convicted, he was looking at seven years in prison, but he got off easy and only served ten days.

4. Sometimes jail would be preferable.

Kyle Falconer is the singer for a Scottish band called the View. Falconer got collared with some coke after a gig and dutifully coughed up the £1,000 fine. But that wasn't the end of the band's financial woes—during the court case, Falconer's lawyer revealed that the bust had cost the band a £1 million jeans endorsement deal. Oops.

5. Note to David Lee Roth: New York City pot dealers DELIVER

Every weed-smoking New Yorker knows that if you want weed, you find someone who knows someone—someone who'll pedal their bike over to your home, office, or swank rock-star hotel room with a variety of quantities and qualities to choose from. It's as easy as ordering Chinese food, which you'll probably also do after a couple bong hits. But in 1993, Van Halen's David Lee Roth was popped by the cops in Washington Square Park by an undercover police officer selling him $10 worth of crappy Jamaican shake.

6. Boy George calls cops to his own coke-filled apartment.

Though his arrest for chaining up a rent boy and then beating the poor guy with a dildo was bad, George O'Dowd's lamest brush with the law came when he called the cops on himself. Presumably addled out of his mind on drugs, he called 911 to report a burglary in progress. When the cops arrived, they didn't see any robbers, but they couldn't help but notice a pile of blow right out in plain view. Naturally, George claimed the powder was not his (perhaps it belonged to the imaginary burglar?), but a judge didn't believe him and he was sentenced to street-cleaning detail.

7. Good ol' boy turns snitch.

When Gregg Allman was arrested on federal drug charges, he decided he'd rather not go to jail and instead made a deal to testify against a friend of the band's instead. Understandably, this cowardly behavior didn't go down well with those around him and he was shunned by his bandmates for a couple years until the rest of the guys decided they needed money more than they needed to take a moral stand.

8. Donovan was an early adopter.

There've certainly been bigger busts, but bluesy singer Donovan can lay claim to being the first big-time Brit to be busted for marijuana possession. This happened in 1966 and as a result, he wasn't allowed into the US until 1968. By then I guess everyone figured they had bigger bands to fry.

9. Punishment doesn't necessarily fit the crime.

When Freddie Fender and his bass player were busted for possession of two joints, I'm sure they were worried, but not *that* worried. But it was 1960 and they were Latin and in the South and so Freddie was sentenced to *three years* in the notorious Angola Prison Farm. Though it was rumored that as a condition of parole Freddie couldn't play music for a few years, he revealed to Terry Gross on NPR, that he was actually only ordered to stay away from places that served alcohol. Yeesh. Two joints, three years?

10. What a difference several decades makes.

Country crooner Willie Nelson is no stranger to being busted for pot and he's an outspoken critic of the drug war, so it was probably no surprise when the cops came a-knockin' on the tour bus door in November of 2010. They arrested everyone on the bus and charged them with possession of 1.5 pounds of pot and several ounces of hallucinogenic mushrooms. Nelson took it all in stride, cheerfully posting the $2,500 bail and reportedly saying, "Both bus drivers were over fifty years old. The other guys were sixty years old. My sister is seventy-five, I'm seventy-three, so it's like they busted an old folks' home."

11. You want my what?

Most men celebrate their midlife crisis with a fast car or an ill-advised affair, but Wham's George Michael has been having his quite publicly and illegally. Whereas most of us got our drunk driving/pot smoking/public sexing out of our systems in our teens and twenties, George is passing out in his car, then drunkenly/stonily crashing his Range Rover into a photo shop (called Snappy Snaps!), getting picked up while trying to pick up men in park bathrooms, and being nabbed with crack and pot in yet another public toilet.

HONORABLE MENTIONS

Rolling Stones at Redlands

Various Rolling Stones have been arrested over the years on a variety of charges, most of them drug-related. But the most notorious bust took place in 1967 at Keith Richards's Redlands estate. Jagger and Richards were sentenced to three and twelve months, respectively, but their sentences (not convictions) were thrown out on appeal. At the time, much was made of Marianne Faithfull's presence—she was found nude, save for a fur bedspread, and, some said, a Mars bar lodged up her rectum. Keith Richards and others now refute the candy-bar story, making this drug bust far less fun.

Big Buster

Sargeant Norman Pilcher busted Donovan and the Beatles' John Lennon and George Harrison on pot charges. He also orchestrated the famous Rolling Stones Redlands bust. The people he arrested often complained that he was planting the drugs he'd "found," and indeed, he was convicted of perjury in 1973.

13 PUNK ROCK HEROIN ODS

1. GG Allin

Though GG was always promising to kill himself onstage, he wound up buying the farm by way of accidental overdose after a gig in 1993.

2. Dimwit, aka Ken Montgomery (D.O.A.)

Dimwit wasn't a junkie, which is why the nearly pure China White he dabbled with killed him so quickly. He was buried wearing his favorite sweater, clutching his drumsticks and a cookie.

3. and 4. Will Shatter and John Dougherty (Flipper)

Dougherty was brought in to replace Shatter after the former died of a heroin overdose. Dougherty ODed on Halloween, 1997.

5. Delphine Neid (Nuns)

In 1978, the Nuns and the Avengers opened for the Sex Pistols on that band's final show ever and the Nuns have been playing off and on ever since. Alejandro Escovedo was their guitarist and songwriter during the 1970s and Delphine was their bassist until she took too much of the heroin in 1990.

6. Eddie Kurdziel (Redd Kross)

Redd Kross was always a fun, funny punk band, so it's kind of understandable that they unofficially broke up for almost ten years after guitarist Kurdziel's sad demise.

7. Billy Murcia (New York Dolls)

Alcohol + drugs + stupid companions + bathtub = death.

8. Bradley Nowell (Sublime)

Nowell's death proved that shooting up a bunch of dope on the eve of your band's major-label debut is a really fucking stupid thing to do. In case you were wondering....

9. Charlie Ondras (Boss Hog, Unsane)

Ondras was a founding member of both Unsane and Boss Hog until his death in 1992. To honor their fallen friend, Jon Spencer and Cristina Martinez named their first kid Charlie.

10. Malcolm Owen (the Ruts)

The music world was still going nuts over Ian Curtis's death when the Ruts' Malcolm Owen died of an accidental overdose. Much as Darby Crash's death was overshadowed by John Lennon's, Owen's passing was pretty much ignored.

11. Dee Dee Ramone

Shouldn't it be covered in Junkie Business 101 that when you've been clean for a while, you need to adjust your dosage accordingly? That your tolerance goes down according to how long you've been heroin-free? Well, Dee Dee, like so many others, must've skipped this class because that's what happened. Clean system, same old dose, dead Dee Dee.

12. Johnny Thunders

Nobody knows what happened to Johnny Thunders and we probably never will. Some say he was murdered with a hot shot, but the coroner was ready to write him off as just another junkie OD.

13. Sid Vicious, aka John Ritchie

Mother-of-the-year Anne Beverley not only paid for the heroin that killed her son the night he got out of jail, but she allegedly smuggled it into the clink by jamming it up into her baby maker. Mommy Dearest, indeed.

3 PUNK ROCK SUICIDES VIA DRUGS

When these three guys decided it was time to go, they didn't fuck around.

1. Darby Crash

The Germs front man was only twenty-two when he decided to end it all. Unfortunately, his "blaze of glory" was extinguished by the murder of John Lennon the following day.

2. Robert Quine

After Voidoid guitarist Robert Quine's wife suddenly died, he seemingly lost his will to live. Richard Hell wrote in *New York* magazine, "He would tell you how he'd gotten the crying down to two hours a day from four." But less than a year after her death, he loaded up a syringe with a huge amount of heroin and laid down to die.

3. Dave Insurgent, aka Dave Rubenstein (Reagan Youth)

Even if you're not hopelessly addicted to heroin, having your dad run over your mom in a freak accident and then your girlfriend turn out to be the final victim of a serial killer would be a lot to handle. Both these instances happened within a month and Dave couldn't take it and overdosed on sleeping pills.

45 ROCK 'N' ROLL HEROIN DEATHS

Most of these deaths were simple overdoses, but some (as noted) were the result of the body shutting down after years of abuse, or the result of what happens when you hang out with the wrong bunch of people. See? Your mom was right about falling in with the wrong crowd.

1. West Arkeen (songwriter for Guns N' Roses)

Arkeen was badly burned when his barbecue grill exploded all over him. He'd been supplementing his prescribed pain relievers with heroin when he ODed.

2. Chet Baker (crooner/trumpet player)

All doped up, Chet either jumped or fell out an Amsterdam hotel window.

3. Florence Ballard (Supremes)

Ripped off by her record company and treated like crap by Diana Ross, Flo descended into drug abuse and eventually suffered a heart attack brought on by the drugs.

4. Dave Bidwell (Chicken Shack, Savoy Brown, Pink Faeries)

You'd think watching your husband die of an OD would scare you at least straight*ish*, but Biddwell's widow Patty succumbed of the same thing a little while after his death.

5. Mike Bloomfield (the Butterfield Band)

Nobody wants a corpse at their party, so when Mike up and ODed at a friend's bash, two thoughtful guests dragged his body out to their car, drove around for a while, and dumped him off to be found by the authorities later.

6. Tommy Bolin (James Gang, Deep Purple)

The guitarist was only twenty-five years old when he ODed on heroin, alcohol, cocaine, and barbiturates.

7. Tim Buckley

Buckley was allegedly able to keep his heroin habit under control while he was out on the road, but when he returned home the last time and mixed his pre-tour dose with a bunch of booze, he died. Sadly, his talented son Jeff also died at a young age.

8. Sonny Clark (hard bop pianist)

Clark played with Anita O'Day, Stan Getz, John Coltrane, and many other jazz greats. He died at thirty-one, of a heart attack caused by years of hard drinking and drugging.

9. Brian Cole (the Association)

Bassist Cole was only twenty-nine when he died, leaving behind three sons. One of the three, Jordan, is now a vocalist and plays keyboards, guitar, and drums with his dad's band.

10. Jesse Ed Davis (Taj Mahal)

Known as a "guitarist's guitarist," Davis played with all the blues greats—John Lee Hooker, B. B. King, Eric Clapton, and many others. Felled by a debilitating stroke in 1988, he died of a heroin overdose shortly thereafter.

11. Howie Epstein (Tom Petty and the Heartbreakers)

His heroin issues not only cost him his gig with the Heartbreakers, dope also ended his life in 2003.

12. Rick Evers (songwriter, once married to Carole King)

About a year after Rick and Carole married, he died of a heroin overdose. Though she'd been married twice before, this loss shook her and the star retreated from the spotlight for a few years to recover.

13. Eyedea, aka Micheal Larsen

Underground MC/singer Eyedea was only twenty-nine when his mom found him dead of opiate intoxication.

14. Pete Farndon (the Pretenders)

The bassist passed out in the bath and drowned after taking too much heroin.

15. Miss Christine Frka (GTO's)

Often credited with creating her boyfriend Alice Cooper's look, Miss Christine was also the cover model for Frank Zappa's *Hot Rats* album.

16. Jerry Garcia

Though the official cause of death was heart attack, the Grateful Dead leader was in rehab trying to kick his longtime heroin habit.

17. Paul Gardiner (Tubeway Army)

Bandleader Gary Numan paid tribute to his fallen friend with the extremely sad song "A Child with the Ghost."

18. Gidget Gein, aka Bradley Stewart (Marilyn Manson)

Best known for his bass playing with Marilyn Manson, Gein was also a talented painter and writer. Like so many others who went before him, he was in the process of kicking dope when it kicked him.

19. Sean Greenway (GOD)

The Aussie punk band GOD was best known for their song "My Pal" before squabbles split them up, and the Yes Men looked like they were on the verge of making it when Greenway went bye-bye in 2001. Tim Hemensley, another original member of GOD, ODed two years after his former bandmate.

20. Dwayne Goettel (Skinny Puppy)

Skinny Puppy were almost as well known for the insane amount of drugs they ingested as they were for their dark industrial sound, so it was sad, but not completely surprising, when Goettel passed.

21. Stacy Guess (Squirrel Nut Zippers)
Guess's habit got him kicked out of Squirrel Nut Zippers after their first album, and even though he went to rehab, Guess never really quit using. He ODed at thirty-two, in 1998.

22. Tim Hardin (folkie)
Was it pleurisy or heroin that caused Hardin to fall asleep onstage at the Royal Albert Hall? Nobody's sure, but they do know it was the drugs that killed him in 1980, at age thirty-nine.

23. Tim Hemensley (GOD)
Having a second band member die means there'll never be a reunion tour for this loud, punky, fun Melbourne band.

24. Janis Joplin
Joplin was the Amy Winehouse of her generation.

25. John Kahn (Jerry Garcia Band)
I imagine being in the Dead or one of their offshoots is like walking around in a hazy cloud of stinky weed and crazy psychedelics. Except despite their reputation for using softer drugs, both Garcia and his bassist died from the hard stuff.

26. Kenny Kirkland (keyboardist/pianist)
The talented pianist played with a laundry list of stars, including Youssou N'Dour, Joni Mitchell, and Crosby, Stills, Nash and Young, but was probably best known for his stint playing with Branford Marsalis in *The Tonight Show with Jay Leno* house band.

27. Frankie Lymon
"Why Do Fools Fall in Love" (with heroin)? Lymon was only twenty-five when he was found dead in his granny's bathroom.

28. Phil Lynott
The Thin Lizzy front man died from heart failure brought on by years of heroin addiction.

29. Liam Maher (Flowered Up)
Though his overdose wasn't ruled a suicide, the Flowered Up front man had eight times the lethal dose of dope in his system.

30. David McComb (Triffids)

You'd think that having a heart transplant might scare you straight (especially when your heart problems were drug-related), but McComb continued his regimen of drinking and drugging after surgery. His official cause of death was a combination of heroin toxicity and the fact that his body was rejecting the heart transplant he'd just had.

31. Jimmy McCulloch (Wings, Small Faces, the Dukes)

Thou he was best known for his stint with Paul McCartney's Wings, the Scottish guitarist was extremely prolific, playing with Peter Frampton, the reunited Small Faces, and many others. He was only twenty-six when he died of heart failure caused by too much heroin.

32. Robbie McIntosh (Average White Band)

This isn't the guitarist Robbie McIntosh who played with the Pretenders. That bloke's still among us. This Robbie was a drummer who croaked after snorting a bunch of powder he mistakenly believed to be cocaine.

33. Jonathan Melvoin (Smashing Pumpkins)

Melvoin was partying with Pumpkins drummer Jimmy Chamberlain when he bought the farm via a fatal dose of powerful heroin with the street name "Red Rum." Ironically, Red Rum was also the name of one of Melvoin's side projects. Ironically times two, Melvoin's father was the founder of MusicCare's Substance Abuse Initiative, an outreach group designed to help musicians fight drug abuse.

34. Joachim Nielsen, aka Jokke (lead singer of Norway's Jokke and Valentinerne)

It's difficult to resist making a joke when the guy goes by Jokke, but I'll refrain.

35. Gram Parsons

Mixing heroin and alcohol is never a good idea.

36. Dickie Pride, aka Richard Charles Knellar

This British one-hit wonder was devastated, and unable to recover, when his success only lasted a week and he was dropped from Larry Parnes's stable of artists.

37. Gary Primich (blues harmonica player)

Best known for his album, *Mr. Freeze*, this Austin Hall of Famer succumbed to smack in 2007.

38. Jason Rae (saxophone player, spouse of Corinne Bailey Rae)

While his wife's image remains squeaky clean, Jason was known for being a party boy. An accidental OD got him in 2008.

39. John Baker Saunders (Mad Season)

The so-called grunge supergroup was founded after a rehab meet-up between Saunders and Pearl Jam's Mike McCready and fell apart because of drugs. Bassist Saunders and vocalist Layne Staley both ODed.

40. Bobby Sheehan (Blues Traveler)

The bass player died from a fatal cocktail of heroin, cocaine, and Valium.

41. Hillel Slovak (Red Hot Chili Peppers)

Guitarist Slovak, bassist Flea, and singer Anthony Kiedis had been friends since high school, so Slovak's death nearly decimated RHCP. (Fear not—they recovered and are kazillionaires now.)

42. Layne Staley (Alice in Chains, Mad Season)

One of the grimmer rock ODs. Staley was a mess for years before his two-weeks-dead body was discovered. Autopsy reports also say he had cocaine and codeine in his system.

43. Lenny Sullivan (Bruce Springsteen and the E Street Band tour manager)

Springsteen runs a pretty clean ship, so it was surprising when his tour manager turned up dead of acute amphetamine and heroin intoxication.

44. Andrew Wood (Mother Love Bone)

Three days after he was found comatose from an OD, Wood died, so, like Sublime, the band's major-label debut was a posthumous one.

45. Paula Yates (TV presenter, music journalist, married to Bob Geldof, had a child with Michael Hutchence)

Though her death was ruled an accident, Yates was distraught over Hutchence's death and her ongoing custody battle.

THE 3 MOST ENDEARINGLY SLEAZY THINGS ERIC DAVIDSON EVER HEARD AT A ROCK 'N' ROLL WAKE: DEAD BOYS SINGER STIV BATORS'S WAKE, BABYLON A GO-GO, LAKEWOOD, OHIO, 1990

Since it took place in a suburb of Cleveland, a few celebs couldn't drag their fancy asses to the wake for the infamously self-flagellating punk singer. So they sent videos, which were projected for all to watch, including Bators's kindly old Polish parents.

1. I believe John Waters mentioned Bators's penis size.
2. In Iggy Pop's vid-note, he started to cry while saying that "everyone said Stiv ripped me off. But he was the real fuckin' deal…."
3. But by far the best, was Lydia Lunch's heartfelt eulogy:
   "The first time I met Stiv, I was in a cab on the Lower East Side. It stopped, and Stiv just jumps in. We drove a little, and then I gave him a big blow job. Stiv was the best."

18 PRESCRIPTION DRUG OVERDOSES

Illegal drugs aren't the only kind that can kill you—as these examples will show you, there are plenty of ways to off yourself right in your medicine cabinet. Especially if you also have a liquor cabinet.

I. Lester Bangs

Darvon, Valium, and *Nyquil*. Yes, "The nighttime sniffling, sneezing, coughing, aching, stuffy head fever, so-you-can-rest medicine," was partially responsible for offing the great Lester Bangs.

2. Jay Bennett (Wilco)

Died from an accidental overdose of the potent synthetic narcotic Fentanyl.

3. Carl Crack (Atari Teenage Riot)

With a name like "Crack," you'd think it'd be rock that did him in. Nope. Booze and a variety of prescription pills.

4. Erik Brødreskift (Borknagar, Gorgoroth, and Immortal)

Also known as "Grim," the Norwegian black metal drummer killed himself with a handful of pills. The band Nargaroth wrote a song called "Erik, May You Rape the Angels," as a touching tribute to their fallen friend.

5. Chad Butler, aka Pimp C

Popular among a certain breed of Southern hip-hop artist, "syrup" is a mixture of prescription codeine-based cough syrup and something sicky sweet like candy. Unfortunately for Pimp C, this in concert with the rapper's sleep apnea meant an early good night. Ironically enough, Pimp C was a champion of the ultimately fatal beverage and was featured on the 2000 Three 6 Mafia song that brought the practice its first bit of attention, "Sippin' on Some Syrup."

6. Vic Chesnutt

The life of a paraplegic can't be an easy one and at forty-five, the much admired musician finally succeeded—after at least three previous attempts—in killing himself by downing a bunch of muscle relaxers.

7. Nick Drake

Was mope-rocker Drake trying to kill himself when he swallowed a bunch of antidepressants? Or was he just trying to feel better? The coroner thought suicide, but friends and family remain divided.

8. Brian Epstein

The Beatles were obviously in the midst of their obnoxious, hippy-dippy guru stage when their longtime manager died of an accidental overdose of sleeping pills, because John Lennon had this to say: "Our meditations have given us confidence to stand such a shock." Nice. The guy who discovered your overrated asses kicks it and all you offer is new age jabber.

9. Steve Foley (Replacements)

The drummer had been sober for fifteen years when he ODed on drugs used to treat his depression and anxiety.

10. Adam Goldstein, aka DJ AM

Before he nearly died in a plane crash with Blink 182's Travis Barker, Goldstein had been clean and sober for eleven years. Maybe it was the pain meds he needed to cope with his burns, but shortly after filming a brief series on addiction for MTV, he was found dead of an overdose of nearly a pharmacy's worth of drugs, including cocaine, levamisole, oxycodone, hydrocodone, lorazepam, clonazepam, alprazolam, and diphenhydramine.

11. Paul Gray (Slipknot)

The masked bass player croaked from combining synthetic morphine (Fentanyl) with the real thing.

12. Michael Jackson

His death has been ruled a homicide, but Jackson had been a fan of the drugs for years. He had an on-staff physician administer a heavy sedative called propofol. Normally when the drug is administered, it's in a hospital with someone monitoring the patient's breathing. Not so at Neverland, and so Jackson's doctor is up on charges.

13. Gerald Levert

The R&B singer died from "accidentally" ingesting most of the contents of your local CVS. The coroner ruled his cause of death as "acute intoxication of Percocet, Vicodin, Darvocet, Xanax, and two antihistamines."

14. Billy Mackenzie (the Associates)

Sadness over his mother's death drove Mackenzie to walk out to his family's shed and swallow a lethal dose of assorted pills. The singer was much mourned among his colleagues: The Cure and Siouxsie and the Banshees both wrote songs about his death, while the Smiths had two hits based on Mackenzie's friendship with Morrissey.

15. Keith Moon

How ironic (and horrible) is it that Keith Moon overdosed on the seizure meds he was taking to control his alcoholism? (That's a rhetorical question.)

16. Elvis Presley

Much like the King of Pop, the King had an obedient doctor on his payroll. Dr. George C. Nichopoulos had his license suspended for three months (it was eventually yanked) after it was discovered he'd prescribed between 5,000 and 10,000 sedatives in the eight months before Elvis's death. Though the legend's cause of death was listed as cardiac arrhythmia, it's no wonder Elvis the Pelvis's heart was beating funny, with fourteen different drugs coursing through his system. His ticker finally gave out on August 16, 1977, while the King was planted on his throne.

17. Steve Clark

The Def Leppard guitarist only thirty years old when his girlfriend discovered his dead body. Clark was on painkillers for a cracked rib and combined those with antidepressants, morphine, Valium, and three times the legal amount of liquor. The killer combo was ruled accidental.

18. Rob Pilatus

Pilatus, one half of the disgraced "Girl You Know It's True" duo Milli Vanilli, never really recovered from the scandal of being found out as a fraud. He was in and out of rehab in his native Germany, and finally died from a heart attack caused by alcohol and "an unspecified medication." This medication was rumored to be methadone, though that information has never officially been released.

12 KILLED BY COCAINE

Though it's certainly possible to die of cocaine, coke generally puts you in the ground by either giving you a heart attack or hardening your arteries until the life is squeezed out of you.

1. Kevin DuBrow (Quiet Riot)
2. John Entwistle
3. Andy Gibb
4. Bobby Hatfield
5. James Honeyman-Scott
6. Shannon Hoon (Blind Melon)
7. Brent Mydland (Grateful Dead)
8. Jay Reatard
9. David Ruffin (the Temptations)
10. Ike Turner (rock 'n' roll pioneer/wife beater)
11. Jeff Porcaro (Toto)
12. Ol' Dirty Bastard (Though the coke had a little help from all the other drugs in his system.)

7 ROCKERS WHO GAGGED TO DEATH ON THEIR OWN PUKE

Besides autoerotic asphyxiation, choking to death on your own vomit is probably the least dignified way a person can leave this mortal coil. Here are seven notable ones who did.

1. John Bonham

Bonham began the last day of his life with sixteen shots of vodka and continued on until he passed out and was put to bed at Jimmy Page's house after a long day of rehearsals. John Paul Jones found him the next afternoon, asphyxiated on his own sick.

2. Stuart Cable (Stereophonics)

The onetime Stereophonics drummer (hmm, two drummers in a row) was an admitted coke hound, but had cleaned up his act after he was kicked out of the band and moved back to the boonies of Wales. Well, "cleaned up" at least as far as illegal drugs went. His untimely death was the end result of a three-day drinking binge.

3. Eric "Stumpy Joe" Childs

What is it with drummers?! When you have a drummer curse like Spinal Tap did, it's inevitable that one of them is going to go out choking on *somebody's* vomit.

4. Tommy Dorsey

The volatile big-band leader died after popping a couple sleeping pills following a heavy meal.

5. Steven Gately (Boyzone)

After a big night of drinking out at the clubs, Gately's boyfriend woke up to find him crouched on their sofa, dead, his lungs filled with puke.

6. Jimi Hendrix

Sleeping pills and red wine definitely do not mix.

7. Bon Scott

"Acute alcohol poisoning" and "death by misadventure" are apparently British for "gagging to death on your own hurl."

7 POSTHUMOUS RECORDS THAT WERE RELEASED BEFORE RIGOR MORTIS EVEN SET IN

Everyone on this list (except Jeff Buckley) died of drug-related causes, each on the verge of a major release.

1. Michael Jackson, *Michael*

If he could've gotten away with it, Joe Jackson would've been hawking commemorative key chains at Michael's funeral, so it's kind of shocking that he objected to Sony's rush to release this first—of many, I'm sure—posthumous album. Shocking until you realize Creepy Joe was completely cut out of his son's will and doesn't stand to make any dough off of it.

2. Janis Joplin, *Pearl*

Janis was on an upward trajectory when she accidentally ODed. She had a hot twenty-one-year-old boyfriend, a new band, and was allegedly off the hard stuff. Until she wasn't. Four months after her death, *Pearl*, her biggest critical and financial success, was released.

3. Mother Love Bone, *Apple*

The release date for *Apple* (Gwyneth supposedly named her child after this album) was scheduled for a few days after lead singer Andrew Wood took his fatal shot of heroin. The record company waited four months to release it and it was a sales disappointment, though critically acclaimed. It also spawned some of the biggest bands in grunge.

4. Nirvana, *Unplugged in New York*

MTV didn't schedule the release of this album until Kurt was in the ground. It debuted at number one on the Billboard charts and won a Grammy for Best Alternative Record.

5. Gram Parsons, *Grievous Angels*

Gram ODed just a few weeks after finishing this album. The record company waited a respectable four months to release it. Again with the four-month waiting period!

6. Elliott Smith, *From a Basement on a Hill*

After a long back-and-forth with drug addiction, Smith ended his life by stabbing himself in the chest. *From a Basement…*wasn't finished, so his family brought in a producer who completed the job. Ironically, it went on to be one of Smith's best-selling records.

7. Sublime, *Sublime*

The record company almost dumped this record—originally, horribly, called *Killin' It*—after lead singer Brad Nowell ODed two months before its release date. Luckily for the other band members and Nowell's family, the company had a change of heart and the thing went on to sell 6 million copies.

(DIS)HONORABLE MENTION

Just to clarify, Jeff Buckley's death was not drug-related, but his record company's behavior was so egregious that it'll make you want to take drugs. Most of Jeff Buckley's releases have been posthumous, but when he was recording *Grace*, the album that he actually put out while living, he excluded one track, "Forget Her." He said that if he ever heard that song again, he'd "throw up." After he died, the record company completely disregarded his wishes and slapped the song on as an eleventh track on every CD sold after 2004.

ERIC DANVILLE'S 5 FAVORITE ROCK 'N' ROLL SONGS ABOUT LENNY BRUCE

By the time of his death of a heroin overdose in 1966, Lenny Bruce had gone from jazz-cadenced "sick comic" to rock 'n' roll martyr of American hippiedom. After years of drug and obscenity convictions, he'd lost his cabaret card—a license necessary to perform in nightclubs—and could only get gigs in California; his last gig, in 1965, was courtesy of one of his champions, Frank Zappa—who served as opening act for Bruce with the Mothers of Invention and also produced and released the Lenny Bruce album, *The Berkeley Concert*. Bruce was also admired by John Lennon and appeared as one of the many faces on the cover of *Sgt. Pepper's Lonely Hearts Club Band*. Lenny Bruce left behind a daughter, Kitty, an ex-wife, Honey, and an impressive list of rock 'n' rollers willing to sing his praises for years to come. Here are some of my favorites.

I. "Father Bruce," Grace Slick and the Great Society

"Father Bruce" is the first documented and most joyously sike-ay-del-ic rock 'n' roll song about Bruce, written by Grace Slick and members of her pre–Jefferson Airplane band—and probably the only one Lenny might have heard. The tune, like all those that followed, celebrates his life, but to Gracie's credit did so while he was still alive. The lyrics detail Bruce's continued existence after he fell from a San Francisco hotel window while he was playing "Superjew." The Great Society only released one single, so "Father Bruce" didn't drop until the live album, *Conspicuous Only in Its Absence*, did. If Lenny did ever hear this song, he probably appreciated its last line: "Fuck!"

2. "Eulogy to Lenny Bruce," Nico

The former Velvet Underground chanteuse gives the tune—penned by singer/songwriter Tim Hardin, who used to perform it as "Lenny's Song"—a typical mournful quality; but then again, Nico could sing "Frosty the Snowman" and you'd still only think about the day the poor bastard melts. Like most songs about Bruce, "Eulogy" has a very "Why, Lenny? Why?" tone that's totally appropriate, but in this case is compounded by the history of the singer herself, especially in the lines, "Why, after every last shot / Was there always another…?" Hell, having *Nico* mourn your fatal drug OD is kinda like Courtney Love telling Kurt Cobain, "Get thee to rehabbery." In one case it works; in the other, not so much. You decide. In 2000, Sub Pop recording artists Damon and Naomi did their own version on their release *With Ghost*.

3. "Lenny Bruce," Bob Dylan

Ex-hippie protest singer (and Bruce's occasional tribe member) Bob Dylan penned his own eulogy, an oddly emotional tribute that appeared on his 1981 album *Shot of Love*. Driven more by piano than his trademark guitar chording, the song was a rare treat for those who saw Dylan's Never Ending Tour in the early '80s. One part of the song mentions a cab ride Dylan took with Bruce, which must have been a real trip: ("I rode with him in a taxi once / Only for a mile and a half, seemed like it took a couple of months"); these lines were left out when he performed the song with a more gospel feel during his 1986 tour with Tom Petty and the Heartbreakers (as we go to press, the song was performed live 103 times). Dylan also puts out the idea that Lenny's overdose may have been a suicide. If nothing else, it's the first song by Dylan (or anyone else, I'd bet) to mention the Golden Globes and drug-rehab program Synanon in the same line. A more guitar-centric version including strings and keys was performed by former Wall of Voodoo front man Stan Ridgway on his album *Neon Mirage*.

4. "Land of Lenny Bruce," New Toys

The New Toys, a Buffalo, New York–based power-pop punk outfit active from the late '70s to the early '80s, take the world to task for its part in Lenny's death as only a Buffalo, New York–based power-pop punk outfit active from the late '70s to the early '80s could. An obscure and surprisingly toe-tapping song, considering its subject. Definitely worth, uh, tracking down . . .

5. "Big Mouth Strikes Again," Chumbawamba

If anyone would love a drug-taking, establishment-tweaking, controversy-causing comic, it would be this group of anarcho-rockers, who show Bruce the love on their album *Shhh*—whose main theme is censorship. You know things are gonna be great when you hear the opening sample (Robert Plant asking, "Does anybody remember laughter?"). The song features a rap by MC Fusion, singer Alice Nutter's wildly sexy reading of Bruce's "To Is a Preposition, Come is a Verb" routine, and a clip of the man himself. Great stuff. Bruce and Plant were some of the rare samples to make it onto the record; the original album was scrapped when too many artists whose work was nicked objected. Bruce is featured in the upper right-hand corner of the album cover, with his hand covering his mouth.

HONORABLE MENTION

Phil Spector's Last Word

After Bruce was found dead of what was officially called "acute morphine poisoning caused by an accidental overdose," record producer Phil Spector had a different thought on the matter, saying, "Lenny Bruce died of an overdose of police."

When not working his day job as managing editor of *Penthouse Forum* magazine, Eric Danville tells anyone who'll listen that he's the author of *The Complete Linda Lovelace* (Power Process Publishing) as well as *The Official Heavy Metal Book of Lists* (Backbeat Books).

10 REASONS WHY YOU SHOULD ONLY TALK TO THE PRESS WHEN SOBER

I. Because you forget what you said and then freak out when it gets printed

"We went on a binge.... We did a lot of drugs. We got pills and then went to Alphabet City and Kurt wore a hat, I wore a hat, and we copped some dope. Then we got high and went to *S.N.L.* After that, I did heroin for a couple of months." —Courtney Love, in her infamous *Vanity Fair* interview, September 1992

2. Because nobody believes you lost consciousness several times during one interview due to "exhaustion"

"I'm a really big drinker. I used to be there before the pub opened, banging on the door." (Amy Winehouse, in an interview with *Blender*, November 2007. Over the course of this interview she passes out several times and her management tries to blame it on overexertion.)

3. Because it's embarrassing—for you, for the journalist, and for the reader

"No, it increased my appetite for drug abuse! No, you gotta wanna survive. To preserve your life. Maaaybe I just wanna breathe.... You and I are gonna live foreeeever!" (Evan Dando, in an extremely intoxicated chat with *Vox*, November 1996)

4. Because sometimes it's funny and you're not known for your sense of humor

Q: You said a little while ago that you sing mainly about drugs.
A: Sometimes
Q: Why do you do this?
A: 'Cause I think the government is plotting against me.
Q: You like singing about drugs—is this because you like taking drugs yourself?
A: No, it's 'cause I can't carry when I go through customs and I figure someone in the audience...
Q: You want people to take drugs themselves?
A: Oh yeah, I want them to take drugs.
Q: Why's this?

A: 'Cause it's better than Monopoly.
(Lou Reed in a 1974 televised interview with Australian reporters)

5. Because border crossings will be a bitch for the rest of your life

"Over the next three hours, Doherty will also smoke crack, shoot heroin, and take an ecstasy pill. He does all of this casually, and openly, except for the shooting up, which he performs near the kitchenette, with his back to us. He offers me heroin and ecstasy but not crack. I decline. The more drugs Doherty does, the more he seems to relax. He never becomes incoherent, though occasionally he seems confused." (*Rolling Stone* reporter Mark Binelli recounting his 2006 interview with Pete Doherty)

6. Because YouTube means nobody will ever forget

James Brown's loony drunken appearance on *Sonya Live in L.A.* is one of the all-time craziest cautionary tales. The day after he was sprung from jail for assaulting his wife, he got liquored up and decided live TV was the way to go.

Sonya: What are you going to say when your fans ask you some questions about [hitting your wife with a lead pipe]?

King of Soul: I'm gonna say I feel GOOOOOD! Papa's got a brand new bag! It's a man's world! [*Jumps up and throws a few hip thrusts at the camera.*]

7. Because admitting you're high is better than pretending to be crazy

See Paula Abdul's assorted loony drunken/high appearances everywhere from the red carpet to morning news programs. She slurs. She reels. She starts to nod out only to lurch back into consciousness with a nonsensical outburst. Yet Ms. Abdul insists she's never been drunk or high on pills. She attributes her occasional forays into kookooville to the fact that she's "goofy."

8. Because you'll probably blow all your money on booze and hookers and wind up on *Celebrity Rehab* season 5 anyway

Sebastian Bach has been wasted on camera too many times to count. One classic TMZ clip shows him swilling from a bottle of Chianti, taking a hit off a joint, and then barking at the camera, "They ask me every season. I'm not interested in making bad art. *Celebrity Rehab* with Dr. Drew is out of control. That show sucks. That guy's a quack."

9. Because you'll leave people thinking you *should* be on drugs; at least then there's a possibility you'll be entertaining

Though most of Metallica have battled with addiction, they were seemingly sober during the filming of *Some Kind of Monster*. But still, this documentary shows that you really don't want to get personal with most of the people who make the music you love. In addition, watching group therapy is dull even when everyone in the group is famous, and it actually crosses over into infuriating when you realize these guys have more money than you'll ever come close to having and they're still whiny little bitches.

10. Because you could get sued by the four people not smart enough to be embarrassed that they paid money to see Creed

Even worse than being a mess while you're being interviewed is wasting an audience's time by being a drunkard onstage. That's what Creed's Scott Stapp did in Chicago one day in 2002. He was so wasted he slurred what words he could remember and forgot the rest. Four of his fans were so upset they sued the band, though the case was later dismissed. Confidential to those four fans: Dudes, you're going to see *Creed*. Missing the show was a bonus.

17 CAUTIONARY TALES ABOUT HEROIN

1. Dizzy Gillespie
"Cats were always getting busted with drugs by the police, and they had a saying, 'To get the best band, go to Kentucky.' That meant that the 'best band' was in Lexington, Kentucky, at the federal narcotics hospital." (*Milestones*)

2. Mark Arm (Mudhoney)
"Kurt [Cobain] asked me how I managed to stop doing heroin. I told him that I had wanted to, from the depths of my soul. It wasn't fun anymore (it hadn't been fun for a long time), and it was killing me emotionally as well as physically. I guess what I failed to mention was that if you really want to quit, you've got to lose all those junkie leeches you call 'friends' and YOU NEED TO DUMP YOUR JUNKIE WIFE!" (*Thrasher*, Feb. 2001)

3. Jerry Hall

"Mick had told me he took LSD every day for a year in the '60s. He also admitted he was smoking heroin. I was disgusted. I told him I couldn't see him if he took drugs, saying, 'Go away and don't come back until you're straight.' He succeeded—he had amazing willpower." (*NME*, Sept. 27, 2010)

4. Nikki Sixx

"Mick [Mars], our merciless overseer of quality control, bent into the microphone and announced to the assembled mass of businesspeople and dispensers of checks, per diems, and advances: 'Perhaps we could play these songs for you if Nikki hadn't been up all night doing heroin.' I got so pissed off that I threw my bass to the ground, walked over to his microphone, and snapped the stand in half. Mick was already at the door by then, but I chased him down the country lane, both of us in high heels like two hookers in a catfight." (*The Dirt*)

5. Keith Richards

"Sometimes you feel out of sync with the image. I haven't been a junkie for thirty years. I still carry that ball and chain." (From a talk at the New York Public Library, Dec. 29, 2010)

6. Keith Richards, part 2

"I never really overdid it. Well, I shouldn't say *never*; sometimes I was absolutely comatose." (*Life*)

7. Lemmy Kilmister (Motörhead)

"I have never had heroin but since I moved to London in 1967, I have mixed with junkies on a casual and almost daily basis. I hate the idea even as I say it, but the only way to treat heroin is to legalize it." (speaking to the Welsh Assembly, Nov. 3, 2005)

8. Robbie Williams

"When I started going clubbing at sixteen, we were on acid. The acid and speed. Then it progressed into cocaine. Before the acid, heroin. I did that once." (*NME*, Oct. 8, 2009)

9. Paul McCartney

"I didn't realise I'd taken (heroin). I was just handed something, smoked it, then found out what it was. It didn't do anything for me, which was lucky because I wouldn't have fancied heading down that road. I suppose I learnt from an early age to do things in moderation. My dad always used to say 'Don't overdo things. Have a drink but don't be an alcoholic.' That always stuck with me." (*Uncut*, June 2004)

10. Julian Casablancas (the Strokes)

"Doing heroin is like walking around with a terrorist as your friend. It's like taking a terrorist around to parties You never know when it's going to blow up on you." (*Guardian*, Oct. 31, 2003)

11. Malcolm McLaren

"Sid's mother, Anne, was kind enough and helped him wherever she could. A small-time drug dealer, she smuggled heroin in her vagina to Sid at Riker's Island, a detention center in New York where he was awaiting trial for the murder of Nancy. A dutiful mother, she aided him in his last breath, killing him, and killing herself years later." (*Daily Beast*, Feb. 4, 2009)

12. Steve Jones (Sex Pistols)

My fondest memory of Malcolm, and I loved the guy, was his birthday gift to me when I turned twenty-one—he got me a hooker and some heroin." (From a statement released on Malcolm McLaren's death)

13. Eugene Hütz (Gogol Bordello)

"A lot of people are convinced I'm a heroin junkie. I've actually never done that many drugs in my life. I've not done many drugs in my life. It's all adrenaline and music and a bit of alcohol." (*NME*, June 25, 2007)

14. Ryan Adams

"There are the ghosts of about 45 speedballs from when I was recording here a year or two ago…. Without exaggerating, it is a miracle I did not die. I snorted heroin a lot—with coke. I did speedballs every day for years. And took pills. And then drank. And I don't mean a little bit. I always outdid everybody." (*New York Times*, June 17, 2007)

15. Charlie Watts

"I had a pretty bad midlife crisis I went through. But I have a phobia of needles, so I could not exactly be a junkie. Even now, I am *awful* if I have to have injections. So I could not sit and do it to myself, like I've seen other people do. I mean, I have taken drugs that were a waste of money, because I didn't do it properly and I wasn't interested, either. But you know, that's growing up, isn't it?" (*Details*, Mar. 2010)

16. Dr. John

"I remember going into the high school, the first time I got really loaded, and I walked up these stairs and puked all over this trophy case, and I thought, 'This is what being high is all about.' I felt so good. And that was the high I chased all my life." (*The Harder They Fall*)

17. Chuck Negron (Three Dog Night)

"I don't know why I stayed alive. I used dirty needles. Four people were beaten to death with baseball bats at an upscale heroin shooting gallery in Laurel Canyon.... [T]he carnage happened in the very place I was spending most of my evenings at the time—except that murderous one." (*The Harder They Fall*)

THE LIGHTER SIDE

11

RICHARD MANITOBA'S 9 BEST DRUGS EVER (IN DESCENDING ORDER)

1. Heroin

Best drug ever. No matter what drug they invent, what I might have missed—because there are a plethora of new intoxicants all the time—I went out with a World Championship ring on my finger. I went out winning the World Series and I retired in 1983. Heroin was the granddaddy of them all.

But along with it being best-feeling drug of all time, it was probably the worst choice I could've made. I have an addictive personality and I was in my teens, trying to figure out how to negotiate life—this was the opposite of what I needed in order to survive. Resilience and toughness are tools you need to get by in life; heroin smooths it all out and gives you the feeling that everything's all right, even when it's not. The first time I ever did it, I threw my guts up. After that, most people would say "ugh." I said, "I want more."

I think of heroin as a cartoon of the gorgeous, seductive woman in the bikini, who you're reaching for—because that's how good it feels going in—but then as soon as you grab her (or heroin grabs you), she turns into a skeleton version of that, laughing at you.

If I've learned nothing else, it's that you're going to get your ass kicked. You need to learn how to survive, and heroin robs you of that skill, because it turns into the most isolating, hide-from-the-world addiction. You become like a fly, careening toward the bright light. Not thinking, just trying to get to that light.

2. The quaalude family (methaqualone; also known as "ludes," "lemons," "Mandrax," Mandies," "714s," "Paris 700s," "furies," and, by some, "panty droppers")

Quaaludes were, to me, a much nicer, cleaner, easier, smoother, way of getting drunk without all the vomiting. It was a muscle relaxer and it was all over the place in the '70s. I used to buy a thousand and sell them for fifty cents each. You just pop one in your mouth and you're cool, you're a virtual bon vivant (or so you think), and all you wanna do is fuck. It didn't take the work or the time that liquor did and it didn't make you feel physically ill either. You just down a Q and twenty minutes later, you are one happenin' dude.

Mildly dabbled in Valium and other anti-anxiety drugs, but they were not my relaxants of choice.

3. Barbiturates

The "greasers" or the "hitters," as they used to call them, used barbiturates. I'd hang out with them, but I also used to also hang out with the smart kids who were doing hallucinogens and listening to more cutting-edge music. Seconals, Tuinals…they were in that same family of feelings as quaaludes, but they weren't as smooth and polished. Barbiturates were a little more drunky…a little more sloppy. They were a more of a heavy metal drug, while quaaludes were more of a Woodstock thing.

4. Coffee (aka Nectar of the Gods)

The last vice I have left. Can't wait to get to my morning coffee. In the words of my good friend singer/songwriter, Palmyra Delran, "I can't wait to go to sleep, so I can wake up and have my morning coffee." By the way, don't waste your time with decaffeinated—it should be illegal.

5. Booze

The ease of liquor is that it's legal and there's little societal stigma attached to it. If done correctly, as my dad taught me (food in your stomach, good-quality booze, slow pace), it can be a pleasurable experience. There's a fun aspect on the way up because you start drinking with a clear head, but when you make the decision to keep drinking, you're half in the tank, which means that decision is being made by a drunken fool.

6. Cocaine

Cocaine gives you a mediocre buzz, costs a lot of money, and makes you completely socially annoying. However, when taken intravenously it would move way up the list. Unfortunately, you need to keep shooting up every five minutes. However, when mixed with heroin, in a speedball, it's just about the most intense high you can get. Snorted, it just gets caught in your nose hair. Also, some of the creepiest people in Hollywood and the entertainment industry use it. Dirty old men use cocaine to get young girls, which makes it even lamer.

7. Black beauties and speed

The most insane drug of them all. It's probably the most quickly emotionally and physically destructive drug there is. The only reason I dabbled in it at all was because it was right in front of me.

8. Pot

In the early part of my retarded development, I loved it, cherished it, collected it, sold it…I was a purveyor, I was an expert. And then suddenly, unexpectedly, I hated the way it made me feel—nervous, paranoid. It got in the way of getting things done. It slowed me down and made me just want to eat chocolate chip cookies and milk. I gave it up not as something to save my life; I just started to despise it. It's one of the most heinous drugs because it has this reputation of being light and mild, and yet to somebody growing up—who doesn't have a handle on life yet— they can get into it thinking that it's okay because it's mellow and subtle, but that's the insidiousness of it because it's still a drug. It's actually more destructive than people are willing to admit because it's accepted, when in reality it's just another way of not dealing with things. The high you get from it, the whole thing is lame—it's horrible and a complete waste of time. If you're going to do a drug, just do a drug. Do heroin!

9. Psychedelics (LSD, acid, mescaline, mushrooms, etc.)

There are people in the world who believe that if you take a trip and something goes wrong, there's something wrong with *you*. They use this as a litmus test. It's the lamest, stupidest, worst drug ever invented. You have to say, "I'm going to put aside this day, I'm going to take a bunch of hours and go *where*?" As I got older, the contract I signed for how high I wanted to get became more clear—I wanted to know how high I'd get, how long it would last, and when I'd be done. I found it much easier to sign that contract than this open-ended one where I didn't know what kind of high I'd have or when it would be over.

INCOMPLETES

Glue, paint thinner, whip-its, and other over-the-counter, fume-based intoxicants

I never really got into the feeling of getting dizzy from some easy, cheap thing, though I don't know any kid growing up who didn't at least investigate inhalants. The high is not that good versus the millions of brain cells you kill each time you do it. At least with heroin and pot you can go out into the world and function. With this stuff, it's a one-way ticket to Nowheresville Daddy-O.

Mr. Manitoba is the lead singer of the legendary Dictators and owner of Manitoba's, a popular bar on Avenue B in New York City. He also has his own radio show, *The Handsome Dick Manitoba Program*, heard weeknights in Little Steven's Underground Garage on Sirius XM radio. Twenty-seven years ago he realized that while the ascent into drug use was a whole lot of fun, what goes up must come down, and that descent can be ugly, destructive, and brutal, so he quit and has been sober for nearly three decades. He never freebased or experienced drugs like crack or any of the so-called hug drugs, which is why they're not included.

101 SONGS ABOUT HEROIN

Though this list is by no means exhaustive, it was exhausting to discover there were so many songs written about dope.

1. "King Heroin," James Brown
2. "Hand of Doom," Black Sabbath
3. "Junkie," Ozzy Osbourne
4. "Runaway Train," Soul Asylum
5. "The Killing," the Ragga Twins
6. "Smack My Bitch Up," the Prodigy
7. "Heroin," Lou Reed, Velvet Underground, U2, and Sinéad O'Connor
8. "King Heroin," Jazzy Jeff
9. "Dead Flowers," Rolling Stones
10. "Sister Morphine," Rolling Stones

11. "Brown Sugar," Rolling Stones
12. "Monkey Man," Rolling Stones
13. Coming Down Again," Rolling Stones
14. "The Needle and the Damage Done," Neil Young
15. "Tonight's the Night," Neil Young
16. "Junkie Nurse," Royal Trux
17. "Golden Brown," the Stranglers
18. "Jesus Shootin' Heroin," the Flaming Lips
19. "Chinese Rocks," Dee Dee Ramone wrote it for the Ramones, though the Heartbreakers' version was more popular
20. "Call the Doctor," Spacemen 3
21. "Super Stupid" (about cocaine *and* heroin), Funkadelic
22. "Loose Booty," Funkadelic
23. "Not if You Were the Last Junkie on Earth," Dandy Warhols
24. "Junkhead," Alice in Chains
25. "We Were on Heroin," Wasted Youth
26. "Heroin Girl," Everclear
27. "You Are My Heroin," Boy George
28. "We'd Have a Riot Doing Heroin," the Queers
29. "Junco Partner," traditional blues tune performed by the Clash, Dr. John, Professor Longhair, James Booker, and many others
30. "Time Out of Mind," Steely Dan
31. "Mr. Brownstone," Guns N' Roses
32. "Real Live Bleeding Fingers and Broken Guitar Strings," Lucinda Williams
33. "Lonely Junkie," Peter Stampfel and the Bottle Caps
34. "Junker's Blues," Champion Jack Dupree, Fats Domino
35. "Dope Head Blues," Victoria Spivey
36. "Minnie the Moocher," Cab Calloway (opium)
37. "Heroin," Roky Erickson
38. "Carmelita," Warren Zevon, GG Allin and the Murder Junkies
39. "Needle and the Spoon," Lynyrd Skynyrd
40. "O.D.," Vincent Crane's Atomic Rooster
41. "Sick of Being Sick," the Damned
42. "Dancing Barefoot," Patti Smith
43. "Needle of Death," Bert Jansch
44. "Hand of Doom," Black Sabbath
45. "She's like Heroin to Me," Gun Club
46. "Too Much Junkie Business," Johnny Thunders
47. "Get Adicted," the Adicts

48. "The Beast," the Only Ones
49. "Fire and Rain," James Taylor
50. "Running to Stand Still," U2
51. "Bad," U2
52. "Wire," U2
53. "Under the Bridge," Red Hot Chili Peppers
54. "Sam Stone," John Prine, also covered by Laura Cantrell
55. "Hurt," Nine Inch Nails, covered by Johnny Cash
56. "Junkie's Promise," Sonic Youth
57. "Times of Trouble," Temple of the Dog
58. "Comfortably Numb," Pink Floyd
59. "Needle in the Hay," Elliott Smith
60. "Signed D.C.," Love
61. "Dancing on Glass," Mötley Crüe
62. "Kickstart My Heart," Mötley Crüe (about Nikki Sixx's O.D.)
63. "Love in Vein," Skinny Puppy
64. "Cold Turkey," John Lennon
65. "She Talks to Angels," Black Crowes
66. "Horse with No Name," America
67. "Pool Shark," Sublime
68. "Jane Says," Jane's Addiction
69. "There She Goes," the La's
70. "Heroin, She Said," Wolfsheim
71. "Silver Vein," Versus
72. "My Sweet Prince," Placebo
73. "My First Day," Haystak
74. "Beetlebum," Blur
75. "Captain Jack," Billy Joel
76. "Cold Blue Steel and Sweet Fire," Joni Mitchell
77. "Scag," Archie Shepp
78. "China Girl," Iggy Pop, David Bowie
79. "Four Walls," Staind
80. "Aux Enfants de la Chance," Serge Gainsbourg
81. "My Lady Heroine," Serge Gainsbourg
82. "Baltimore Love Song," 50 Cent
83. "Stone Junkie," Curtis Mayfield
84. "Surfin' on Heroin," Forgotten Rebels
85. "Black Balloon," Goo Goo Dolls
86. "Mainliner," Social Distortion

87. "Billy," Bad Religion
88. "Angel," Sarah McLachlan
89. "Master of Puppets," Metallica
90. "Just One Fix," Ministry
91. "She's like a Shot," Cop Shoot Cop (who get bonus points for junkie imagery in their band name)
92. "True Faith," New Order
93. "Adios," Rammstein
94. "I Think I'm in Love," Spiritualized
95. "Mexican Caravan," Butthole Surfers
96. "Junky Dare," Fang
97. "Rhyme and Reason," Dave Matthews Band
98. "In the Blood," Mudhoney
99. "Mutiny in Heaven," the Birthday Party
100. "Smack Jack," Nina Hagen
101. "I'm Waiting for the Man," the Velvet Underground

6 CELEBS GRIT THEIR TEETH AND TALK ABOUT COKE

1. "Funnily enough, in the 1980s I used to cure athlete's foot by pouring cocaine on my toes. They cut the stuff with so much foot powder back then, it was the best treatment you could find if you had an outbreak on the road. The only problem was the price, which was around $3,000 a toe." (Ozzy Osbourne, Britain's *Sunday Times* magazine, Sept. 26, 2010)

2. "The 1975 tour on which we were about to embark was fueled by Merck cocaine." (Keith Richards, *Life*)

3. According to his old tour manager, the reason that Louis Armstrong used to dab his face so frequently with a white handkerchief whilst playing wasn't because he was hot and sweaty under the stage lights. The hankie was dusted in cocaine and every time he wiped his face he'd actually be snorting blow. (Popbitch, Jan. 20, 2011)

4. "I'd remember how it felt to open up an eight ball and look at this amazing white powder and how great I felt. And I'd chop it up, and I'd get out the grinder and get it ready, and I'd have that first toot and feel magnificent. I was bright. I was handsome…and I could do anything and I was sexy. And I was already starting to have that little tumescent response, the little edge of a woody. I'm feeling great here." (Paul Williams, *The Harder They Fall*)

5. "The only story is that drugs are bad and they will kill you. You will become a prostitute or a rapist or a dealer. But that's not true. I know lots of people that take cocaine three nights a week and get up and go to work every day, no problem at all. But we never hear that side of the story." (Lily Allen, the *Word*, Jan. 7, 2009)

6. "Sometimes it really freaks me out…when I think about laying in my apartment with bug bites from bedbugs and roaches on the floor and mirrors with cocaine everywhere and no will or interest in doing anything but making music and getting high." (Lady Gaga, *Rolling Stone*, July 8–22, 2009)

30 SONGS ABOUT COCAINE

1. "Snowblind," Black Sabbath
2. "Lit Up," Buckcherry
3. "Cocaine," JJ Cale
4. "Cocaine Blues," Johnny Cash
5. "Cocaine," Eric Clapton
6. "Life in the Fast Lane," Eagles
7. "CCKMP (Cocaine Cannot Kill My Pain)," Steve Earle
8. "Cocaine," Eminem, featuring Alicia Keys
9. "This Boy," Franz Ferdinand
10. "Ride a White Horse," Goldfrapp
11. "Casey Jones," Grateful Dead
12. "Rest My Chemistry," Interpol
13. "White Lines," Grandmaster Melle Mel
14. "White Horse," Laid Back
15. "Take a Whiff on Me," Leadbelly
16. "Da Blow," Lil Jon

17. "Snakes on Everything," Little Feat (cocaine with a side of hallucinations!)
18. "Pusherman," Curtis Mayfield
19. "Psycho," System of a Down (First line, repeated endlessly: "Psycho! Groupie! Cocaine! Crazy!")
20. "Ayo for Yayo," Andre Nickatina
21. "Gold Dust Woman," Stevie Nicks
22. "Cocaine Sex," Renegade Soundwave
23. "Bales of Cocaine," Reverend Horton Heat
24. "Hustlin'," Rick Ross
25. "The White Lady Loves You More," Elliott Smith
26. "Prangin' Out (Pete and Mike's Version)," the Streets
27. "Cocaine Computer," Trans Am
28. "Heroin and Cocaine," Tiger Lillies
29. "Cocaine," Urban Dogs
30. "Wacky Dust," Chick Webb, with Ella Fitzgerald

10-PIECE CRACK ATTACK

1. "MTV Makes Me Want to Smoke Crack," Beck
2. "The Crack House," Fat Joe
3. "10 Crack Commandments," Notorious B.I.G.
4. "Your Mama's on Crack Rock," the Dogs
5. "Crack Addict," Limp Bizkit
6. "Get Your Mother Off the Crack," Audio Two
7. "Night of the Living Baseheads," Public Enemy
8. "Cabbies on Crack," the Ramones
9. "Gimme No Crack," Shinehead
10. "Crack Music," Kanye West

HONORABLE MENTION

There's a band called Leftöver Crack, which is crazy because if you've ever been around crackheads, you know there are never any leftovers.

9 CRAZY TRIP STORIES

I. When Grace Slick nearly dosed Richard Nixon

"All it takes is a little acid to get you to the moon. Entertainers gesture a lot, and I'll be talking to Tricky [Nixon] and I'd kind of gesture over his teacup and the acid would drop in there and he'd never taste it, and in forty-five minutes, the guy would be gone." (*New York Times*, Sept. 20, 1998)

2. Raekwon is not down with the hug drug.

"I never liked ecstasy. All it is is like mescaline for the new millennium. It's just another upper. It's like a damn Anacin…. Yeah, an Anacin with a little bit of Hennessy on top." (*Vice*, Feb. 2001)

3. Shock of the century: Jerry Garcia enjoyed ingesting psychedelics.

"Psychedelics were probably the single most significant experience in my life. Otherwise I think I would be going along believing that this visible reality here is all that there is. Psychedelics didn't give me any answers. What I have are a lot of questions. One thing I'm certain of; the mind is an incredible thing and there are levels of organizations of consciousness that are way beyond what people are fooling with in day-to-day reality." (*Mavericks of the Mind*)

4. Even goths like acid.

"I have never had a bad trip, never. It does set you off though, you take other drugs at the wrong time at the wrong moment and it does set me off again. Some of my younger nephews and nieces say, 'Come on uncle Robert, have a bit of this.' And I'm like, 'Oh yeah, all right,' and then I'm like, 'Fuck!' I'm sitting there an hour later and they're going 'Are you all right?' 'What?'" (the Cure's Robert Smith talking about all the LSD he ingested to write *Disintegration*, *NME*, Oct. 29, 2008)

5. It helped push Syd Barrett over the edge, though.

"It was a huge shock, because I hadn't seen him for about six years. He kept standing up and brushing his teeth, putting his toothbrush away and sitting down. Then at one point he stood up and said, 'Right, when do I put the guitar on?' And of course he didn't have a guitar with him. And we said, 'Sorry Syd, the guitar's all done.'" (Roger Waters, interviewd in *Mojo*, May 1994)

6. If you don't believe me, please translate Syd's ramblings . .

"I only know the thing of playing, of being a musician, was very exciting. Obviously, one was better off with a silver guitar with mirrors and things all over it than people who ended up on the floor or anywhere else in London. The general concept, I didn't feel so conscious of it as perhaps I should. I mean, one's position as a member of London's young people's I dunno what you'd call it underground wasn't it wasn't necessarily realised and felt, I don't think, especially from the point of view of groups." (*Melody Maker*, Mar. 27, 1971)

7. Brent Hinds of Mastodon is an unabashed acidhead.

"Acid is the best drug in the world. It did the most amazing things for my creative psyche, and it still is doing it for me." (*Rolling Stone*, Feb. 17, 2011)

8. Er, Henry Rollins—weren't you supposed to be straight edge?

"Tried LSD. Interesting. Can lose your mind. Something told me, 'you're not doing this anymore,' and I said, 'right' and I didn't." (PopEntertainment.com)

9. More stating the obvious: The "acid house" movement involved a heavy intake of psychedelics (though they did come up with a few new ones).

Phil Hartnoll (Orbital): "It definitely came together, the drugs and the music as part of the same package. If you look back through history, new music is quite often associated with a new drug, isn't it?" ("Second Summer of Love," the *Observer*, Apr. 2008)

13 BANDS THAT MAY (OR MAY NOT) BE NAMED AFTER PSYCHEDELICS

1. Blue Cheer
2. Rich Kids on LSD
3. Hallucinogen
4. Left Spine Down
5. LSD Pond
6. 1200 Micrograms (sometimes called 1200 Mics)
7. L.S.D. Orkestrasi
8. Kaotic Chemistry
9. Love Spirals Downwards
10. Lords of Acid
11. Tripping Daisies
12. Psychedelic Furs
13. XTC

25 PSYCHEDELIC PSONGS

There are literally thousands of songs designed to be listened to while you've got a brainful of blotter. For example, anything Pink Floyd has ever committed to vinyl, especially during the Syd Barrett years. Jefferson Airplane, King Crimson, the Byrds…There are dozens of these bands. And Christ on a crutch, who could possibly enjoy the Grateful Dead with even the vaguest grasp of their faculties? Here we've whittled it down to twenty-five—a starter selection for the newbie tripper.

1. "Lucy in the Sky (With Diamonds)," the Beatles
2. "Space Oddity," David Bowie
3. "Hallucinations," Tim Buckley
4. "Eight Miles High," the Byrds
5. "Psychotic Reaction," Count Five
6. "Fire," the Crazy World of Arthur Brown
7. "White Room," Cream
8. "Season of the Witch," Donovan
9. "The End," the Doors
10. "I Had too Much to Dream Last Night," Electric Prunes
11. "My Fault," Eminem
12. "Maggot Brain," Funkadelic
13. "Dark Star," Grateful Dead
14. "Are You Experienced," Jimi Hendrix
15. "In-A-Gadda-Da-Vida," Iron Butterfly
16. "White Rabbit," Jefferson Airplane
17. "Moonchild," King Crimson
18. "I Walk on Guilded Splinters," Dr. John
19. "She Comes in Colors," Love
20. "Electrallentando," H. P. Lovecraft
21. Anything Pink Floyd has ever released
22. "Shine on Brightly," Procol Harum
23. "Incense and Peppermints," the Strawberry Alarm Clock
24. "I've Got Levitation," 13th Floor Elevators
25. "I Can See for Miles," the Who

9 SONGS (AND 1 ALBUM) ABOUT THE HUG DRUG

1. *It's Great When You're Straight Yeah*, Black Grape
2. "Ecstasy," Bone Thugs-N-Harmony
3. "Everything Starts with an 'E'," E-Zee Possee
4. "24 Hour Party People," Happy Mondays
5. "X," Ja Rule, featuring Missy Elliott and Tweet
6. "Loaded," Primal Scream
7. "Sorted for E's and Wizz," Pulp
8. "Let It Roll," Raze Presents Doug Lazy
9. "I've Lost Control," Sleezy D
10. "Pop a Pill," Young Buck

13 GREAT FILMS WHERE MUSIC MEETS MARY JANE

1, 2., and 3. The Friday Franchise: *Friday, Next Friday,* and *The Friday After Next*

Like most flicks that are made and remade, the original *Friday* is still the best, though a green day spent doing bong hits and watching all three might be a sweet way to spend a Saturday. Rapper Ice Cube is hilarious as the slacker pothead, his misadventures showing the lighter side of hood life.

4. *Detroit Rock City*

When your mom destroys your Kiss tix, what choice do you have but to dose your local priest with magic mushrooms via pizza, shake your teenage ass for Shannon Tweed and a roomful of cougars, and do everything in your power to get enough dough to pay that scalper?

5. *Half Baked*

This hilarious Tamra Davis–directed/Dave Chappelle–cowritten movie features a who's-who of musically inclined stoner cameos by, among others, Snoop Dogg, Willie Nelson, and Tommy Chong.

6. *How High*

Method Man and Redman shoot that "Pot makes you stoopid" propaganda down hard when they discover magical weed that actually makes them smarter and gets them into Harvard. Their logic: Studying while high gives you high grades. Best enjoyed through an *indica* haze.

7. *Nice Dreams*

Who wouldn't enjoy a delicious and refreshing pot-cicle? In Cheech and Chong's third movie, the twosome are dealing weed (and the aforementioned treats) out of an ice-cream truck. Pee-wee Herman shows up, as does Stacy Keach as the dopey cop who keeps trying to bust them. They're dosed by Timothy Leary and hallucinate Jimi Hendrix playing "Purple Haze" (which, BTW, is a strain of MJ).

8. *Rock Opera*

It is impossible to go wrong with a Nashville Pussy soundtrack. That is all.

9. *Soul Plane*

Hilarity ensues when Snoop Dogg's character (he plays the pilot) ODs on magical mushrooms midflight, after smoking a fat blunt in the cockpit. You'll also find Method Man, Tom Arnold(!), and *Precious*'s Mo'Nique onboard the NWA airline's virgin flight.

10. *Hair*

Broadway musicals are, by definition, extremely uncool, but still, this film adaptation was pretty brave for its time. In it, racism, drugs, and anti-war sentiment were served up to the mainstream with a score your mom could tap her toe along with until she actually listened to the words. Though it seems kind of cheesy now, at the time, the film had it all, along with a delicious young Treat Williams playing the lead.

11. *Cheech and Chong's Up in Smoke*

There was a story in the paper recently about a man who smuggled a bag of crack inside his foreskin, but in this 1978 production, Cheech Marin and Tommy Chong got *really* inventive and instead smuggle pot across the border in a van constructed entirely out of the herb. However, the thing this movie's best known for is the Cheech and Chong hit "Earache My Eye," which has been covered extensively by the Rollins Band, Soundgarden, Gov't Mule, and a bunch of others.

12. *Tenacious D in The Pick of Destiny*

Though both Jack Black *and* Kyle Gass passed on being part of this book (and really, Gass—WTF do you have going on?), we decided to let bygones be bygones and include this ode to the sentiment that sometimes dreams really do come true.

13. *The Harder They Come*

Where there's reggae there's weed. Based on a true story, *THTC* features reggae superstar Jimmy Cliff, playing Ivanhoe Martin, a young musician trying to make a name for himself, but who winds up selling weed instead. Things get crazy and he kills a cop, becoming a reluctant folk hero in the process.

9 BANDS NAMED AFTER MARIHOOCH

I. Bongwater
Performance artist Ann Magnuson and Shimmy Disc founder Mark Kramer formed Bongwater in 1985 and lasted for about seven years, releasing four albums and a couple EPs.

2. Bongzilla
Stoner rock from the Land of Cheese (Wisconsin, not France). Aptly enough, they're signed to Relapse Records.

3. Doobie Brothers
"Hey man, got any doobage?" The least appealing band in rock co-opted the least appetizing slang for weed.

4. Green Day
A green day isn't one where you paint your body green and go to a Jets game. Nope, it's when you sit home with an economy-sized bowl of Cheetos, a family pack of Snicker bars, and a big bong packed with righteous weed. Cartoons are on the TV and doing nothing is in the forecast.

5. Kottonmouth Kings
Why would anyone name their band after the most uncomfortable aspect of weed huffing? It's like calling yourself the Paranoia Princess.

6. Marijuana Wolf
Arh-whoooooo!

7. Mary Jane Girls
Rick James put the MJ Girls together, so you *know* there were some drug influences there. The uptight bee-yotches at the PMRC didn't get that their name referenced pot, but gave them the stink-eye over the alleged filth contained in the lyrics to "In My House."

8. Skunk Anansie
They *may* not have been named after skunkweed, as Skin, their lead singer, described their sound as "clit-rock," and everyone knows stoners would rather eat twinkies than puss. We're just happy they reunited.

9. Supergrass

"Caught by the Fuzz" is a catchy tune about a young kid getting nabbed after a drug deal. They *might* not have taken their name from illegal substances, but they sure referenced them in their songs.

5 POT-SMOKING TIPS FROM WILLIE NELSON

I. How you smoke is as important as what you smoke.

"Vaporizers are better for your lungs because you don't inhale any heat and you don't inhale any smoke, you only get the vapors."

2. Practice makes perfect.

"[T]here are stronger strains out there now than there used to be with the old Mexican dirt weed. But I think people have built up their tolerance a lot over the years."

3. If it don't fit, don't force it.

"It's medicine and if it's not your medicine you shouldn't make it so."

4. Just to be clear—pot is not the best thing in the world.

"I don't think I ever said that marijuana is better than sex. If I did, I must've been *really* fucked up. But no, I don't think I ever said that. Marijuana is a nice high, but that's about all you can say about it."

5. Don't waste valuable weed teaching yourself to roll.

"We tried corn silks, cedar bark, coffee grounds, and grapevines before graduating to Bull Durham roll-your-own tobacco, and we did. That's where I learned to roll and why I can roll a joint faster than any living person."

Sources: *The Howard Stern Show, Telegraph* (May 4, 2010), *Vanity Fair* (Aug. 20, 2009), *The Facts of Life and Other Jokes,* by Willie Nelson.

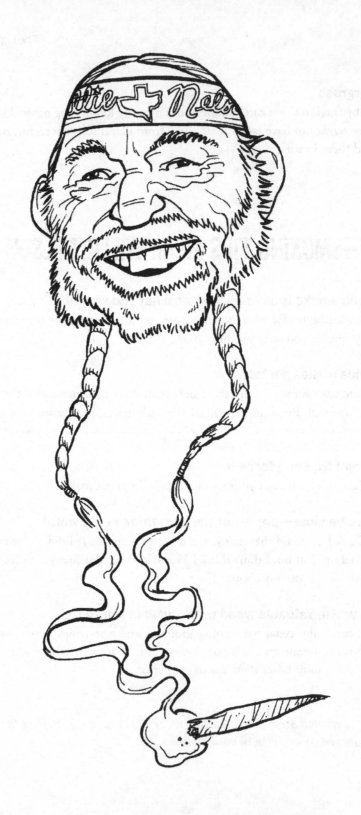

FROM BIG-BAND LEADERS TO PUNK ROCKERS, FROM RAP STARS TO COUNTRY BUMPKINS AND METALHEADS—APPARENTLY, EVERYBODY TRULY MUST GET STONED: 102 SONGS ABOUT POT

1. "Because I Got High," Afroman
2. "Mary Jane," tha Alkaholiks
3. "Alfie," Lily Allen
4. "Muggles," Louis Armstrong
5. "Hold It, Now Hit It," Beastie Boys
6. "I Am the Walrus," the Beatles
7. "Ganja," Bitch and Animal
8. "Sweet Leaf," Black Sabbath
9. "Sinsemilla," Black Uhuru
10. "Buddah Lovaz," Bone Thugs-N-Harmony
11. "Pussy," Brazilian Girls
12. "One Toke over the Line," Brewer and Shipley
13. "Puff Puff Pass," Young Buck
14. "Get High Tonight," Busta Rhymes
15. "Reefer Song," Cab Calloway
16. "Fucked by Northern Lights," Cannabis Corpse
17. "Inhale," Chrome
18. "Seeds and Stems," Commander Cody and His Lost Planet Airmen
19. "I'm in Love with (Mary Jane)," Coolio
20. "Marrakesh Express," Crosby, Stills and Nash
21. "Day 'n' Night," Kid Cudi
22. "Stoned Is the Way of the Walk," Cypress Hill
23. "Brown Sugar," D'Angelo
24. "(Let's Go) Smoke Some Pot," Dash Rip Rock
25. "Drink Beer, Smoke Pot," Dayglo Abortions
26. "Doobie Ashtray," Devin the Dude
27. "Nickel Bag of Funk," Digable Planets
28. "The Next Episode," Dr. Dre
29. "Everybody's Smoking Cheeba," the Donnas
30. "Light My Fire," the Doors
31. "Rainy Day Woman #12 and 35," Bob Dylan

32. "Mr. Tambourine Man," Bob Dylan
33. "Ganja Smuggling," Eek-a-Mouse
34. "Pass That Dutch," Missy Elliott
35. "Dubby Joint," Fatboy Slim
36. "Ganja Babe," Michael Franti
37. "Don't Bogart Me," Fraternity of Man (also Little Feat)
38. "Wake 'n' Bake," the Goats
39. "Texas Tea Party," Benny Goodman and His Orchestra
40. "High Time," Grateful Dead
41. "Knockin' Myself Out," Lil Green
42. "Burnout," Green Day
43. "Burn One Down," Ben Harper
44. "Marijuana," Reverend Horton Heat
45. "Purple Haze," Jimi Hendrix
46. "Mary Jane," Rick James
47. "Blow My Mind," Jamiroquai
48. "Ganja of Love," Jefferson Starship
49. "Reefer Man," Baron Lee and the Blue Rhythm Band
50. "Kronik," Lil' Kim
51. "Lighting Up My Lalala," Lil Wayne
52. "Marijuana in Your Brain," Lords of Acid
53. "Kaya," Bob Marley
54. "One Draw," Rita Marley
55. "Tical," Method Man
56. "The Joker," Steve Miller Band
57. "Big Spliff," Murphy's Law
58. "Pass the Dutchie," Musical Youth
59. "I Smell Smoke," Mystikal
60. "Smokin'," Nas
61. "I'll Never Smoke Weed with Willie [Nelson] Again," Toby Keith
62. "Panama Red," New Riders of the Purple Sage
63. "I Like Marijuana," Mojo Nixon
64. "My Name Is Bud," NOFX
65. "Wacky Tobacky," NRBQ
66. "T.H.C.," Oi Polloi
67. "Flying High Again," Ozzy Osbourne
68. "Crumblin' Erb," OutKast

69. "I Like Marijuana," David Peel
70. "You Don't Know How It Feels," Tom Petty and the Heartbreakers
71. "Pack the Pipe," the Pharcyde
72. "How to Roll a Blunt," Redman
73. "How High," Redman and Method Man
74. "Let's Go Smoke Some Pot," Reel Big Fish
75. "Dope Smokin' Moron," the Replacements
76. "What if God Smoked Cannabis," Bob Rivers
77. "Stoned," Silverchair
78. "Gimme a Reefer," Bessie Smith
79. "If You're a Viper," Stuff Smith and his Onyx Club Boys (renamed "The Reefer Song" in later recordings)
80. "Let's Get Blown," Snoop Dogg and Pharrell Williams
81. "I Love You Mary Jane," Sonic Youth and Cypress Hill
82. "The Way We Get By," Spoon
83. "Bong Hits for Breakfast," Staind
84. "Don't Step on the Grass, Sam," Steppenwolf
85. "I Get High," Styles P, featuring Jadakiss
86. "Light Up," Styx
87. "Smoke Two Joints," Sublime
88. "Stoned if You Want It," Supersuckers
89. "Hydroponic," 311
90. "Bin Laden," Three 6 Mafia
91. "Cheeba Cheeba," Tone Loc
92. "The Pot," Tool
93. "Legalize It," Peter Tosh
94. "Smoke Two Joints," the Toyes
95. "White Punks on Dope," the Tubes
96. "Roll 'Em Up," Vanilla Ice
97. "Light Up or Leave Me Alone," Traffic
98. "High 'Til I Die," 2Pac
99. "Roll Another Number (for the Road)," Neil Young
100. "Champagne and Reefer," Muddy Waters
101. "As High as Wu Tang Gets," Wu Tang Clan
102. "Feelin' It," Jay-Z

BOOZE

12

13 OF THE BIGGEST BOOZERS IN THE HISTORY OF ROCK (IN NO PARTICULAR ORDER)

1. Eddie Van Halen

Though Van Halen's on-again/off-again lead singer, David Lee Roth, was famously quoted as saying, "I used to jog but the ice cubes kept falling out of my glass," Eddie's the drinkingest member of the Van Halen clan, with several stints in rehab (that we know about) under his belt. He told *Hustler* magazine, "I have been drinking, smoking, and playing guitar since I was twelve years old. I still smoke, and I'm definitely playing guitar better than ever. I guess one of the three had to go."

2. Jim Morrison

Morrison's love affair with booze (toward the end, upwards of a fifth a day) was one of the things that helped transform him from the lithe, sinewy Lizard King into the sickly, bloated mess he was when he died. "On a very basic level, I love drinking. But I can't see drinking just milk or water or Coca-Cola. It just ruins it for me. You have to have wine or beer to complete a meal…. Getting drunk…you're in complete control up to a point. It's your choice, every time you take a sip. You have a lot of small choices. It's like…I guess it's the difference between suicide and slow capitulation…. Let's go next door and get a drink." (*Rolling Stone*, July 26, 1969)

3. Warren Zevon

Long before there was a show named *Intervention*, Zevon's friends and family threw one for him. Up until a brief relapse just before his 2003 death (and who wouldn't want a cocktail upon finding out they have just a few weeks to live?) Zevon had been sober for about twenty years. His battle with alcohol was detailed in a grueling *Rolling Stone* story, where he described the physical pain he went through withdrawing. "The last time I detoxed, I really thought I was going to die. I had my hand on the phone, I was afraid that I was going to start hallucinating and shooting guns—I didn't know what was going to happen." (*Rolling Stone*, Mar. 19, 1981)

4. Shane MacGowan

Though the Pogues' MacGowan is one of the reigning poets of our generation, his legacy is probably going to be as patron saint of the severely intoxicated. He told one Irish paper, "There has been more written about how I live my life and what state my health is in than about my music. They've turned me into a drunken monster…. I've got it under control now, I don't drink spirits anymore." As any Pogues show will illustrate, that vow didn't stick. (*Irish World*, Nov. 21, 1997)

5. Keith Moon

Moon was known for his out-of-control behavior—he'd destroy drum kits, blow up toilets, and once even pretended to hijack a plane. Eventually he tried to control his alcoholism with the help of a drug called Heminevrin. His doctor prescribed a hundred pills and, given to excess, Keith took thirty of the sedative at once and died. His good friend Larry Hagman (yes, from TV's *Dynasty*) once said about Moon, "He was a hell of a guy, wonderful. He was smart and funny and talented, but he blew his life out." (*Austin American Statesman*, Mar. 6, 2009)

6. Alice Cooper

"We would go through two, three six-packs each during the day. We always thought we were lightweights 'cause everyone else was doing heroin and cocaine and acid and Quaaludes and we drank beer…. It was always funny to me that groups like Alice Cooper and Black Sabbath—and groups like that—were beer drinkers, and then you would find out that James Taylor and the Monkees and the Mamas and the Papas were junkies. It was just the opposite of what it should have been." (*The Harder They Fall*)

7. Janis Joplin

Though it was heroin that eventually killed her, she was known for rarely being without a bottle of her beverage of choice, Southern Comfort. Her friend and colleague Nick Gravenites describes a typical night at a Joplin gig: "Janis got up. She'd been drinking, she had a bottle up there, she was belting it, she'd just had a fight with a Hells Angel over the bottle of booze, the Hells Angel punched her and took the bottle and another Hells Angel jumped in—it was all real fucking crazy. She was up there singing and she knocked everybody out. She knocked herself out too; 'cause she collapsed too." (*Rolling Stone*, Oct. 29, 1970)

8. and 9. Keith Richards and Ron Wood

As most of the Rolling Stones reached AARP age, there started to be a downturn in the amount of drunken debauchery. Unless you were Keith and Ron, that is. The rest of the band began requesting hotel rooms as far away as humanly possible from the crocked couple, who'd be up all night carousing like crazy.

10. Billy Joel

The man who sang, "Friday night I crashed your party," has been better known lately for drunkenly crashing his car into large, immovable objects like trees or houses.

11. Vince Neil

Vince Neil's drunk driving killed Hanoi Rocks' drummer Razzle and seriously injured the two people in the other car. He spent two weeks in jail, paid the victims' and/or their families $2.6 million, but otherwise walked away unscathed. You'd think that even if he wasn't planning to quit drinking, Neil would at least hire a driver—he can certainly afford one—but nope. He continued drinking and driving and in June of 2010 was busted for it once again.

12. Dusty Springfield

Maybe it was the fact she felt she had to hide her bisexuality from the world, but Dusty was a longtime alcoholic. When she finally dried out, found love, and married, her partner (whom Dusty had met in "the rooms") upset her by sneaking a bottle of champagne into the ceremony. Which, we should mention, was taking place at a fellow AA member's house, and attended by an entirely sober group of people.

13. John Bonham

Bonzo was not a good drunk, even before the booze killed him. A fight with a doorman at L.A.'s Rainbow garnered him fifteen stitches to the cranium, and a dustup with a journalist made all the papers too. His well-known drunken furies prompted one friend of the band to say, "After a while the Beast [Bonham] goes on the prowl and the only thing that amuses him is pillage."

GAY FOR JOHNNY DEPP'S 8 BEST FOOD AND WINE PAIRINGS

1. Chardonnay has gotten a bad rap over the years as the Californians had a bad tendency to "over-oak" this lovely grape and lose out on some of the tropical fruit and herbaceous undertones. But nothing quite pairs with Maine lobster like a fine glass of this full-bodied white wine.

2. Oregon pinot noir always has an earthier tone than its Californian counterpart and this mushroomlike, forest-floor quality pairs perfectly with the heartiness of Alaskan sockeye salmon.

3. Sagrantino di Montefalco, a red wine from Italy's Umbrian region, carries a unique spice and dryness that suits soft creamier cheeses such as taleggio and rich, tomato-based pasta dishes.

4. Tempranillo from Spain is this country's workhorse of a grape and seems to perfectly accompany the peppery spice of much of their cooking by cutting through with round ripe notes of plum and berry.

5. Californian Syrah has a dark cherry character and an intense pepper spice on the sides of the palate that matches well with rosemary-baked lamb shanks.

6. New Zealand's Marlborough region produces unmatched sauvignon blanc that has a grassy nose and hints of citrus in the back of the palate (mostly grapefruit) that goes well with lighter ocean fare such as cod and scallops.

7. Germany's Riesling, a balanced and fruit-forward white, was built for matching with a well-made fondue.

8. And let's not forget France and her stunning Beaujolais wines that have a silky sour-grape quality that is a perfect pairing for holiday dinners that include turkey.

Gay for Johnny Depp are a Brooklyn-based hardcore band with a deep fondness for Mr. Depp. Their latest CD is called *What Doesn't Kill You, Eventually Kills You* and you can find them online at GayforJohnnyDepp.com.

23 ITEMS FOUND IN JANIS JOPLIN'S PURSE (AND NONE OF THEM WERE HEROIN!)

1. Two movie stubs
2. One pack of cigarettes
3. One antique cigarette holder
4. Several motel and hotel room keys
5. One box of Kleenex
6. One compact and various makeup cases (and several eyebrow pencils wrapped in a rubber band)
7. One address book
8. Dozens of bits of paper, business cards, matchbox covers with phone numbers written in nearly illegible barroom scrawls
9. A handful of guitar picks
10. One bottle of Southern Comfort (empty, natch)
11. One hip flask
12. One opened package of complimentary macadamia nuts from American Airlines
13. Cassettes of Johnny Cash and Otis Redding
14. Gum
15. One pair sunglasses
16. Several credit cards
17. Loose aspirin
18. Assorted pens and writing pad
19. One corkscrew
20. One alarm clock
21. One copy of *Time* magazine
22. One copy of Nancy Milford's biography of Zelda Fitzgerald, *Zelda*
23. One copy of Thomas Wolfe's, *Look Homeward, Angel.*

Information garnered from David Dalton's Joplin bio, *Piece of My Heart.*

12 BOOZER BAND NAMES

1. Alcoholic Faith Mission
2. Gallon Drunk
3. Drunk Granny
4. Wasted Youth
5. Everclear
6. Fake ID
7. Free Beer
8. Gin Blossoms
9. Pink Martini
10. Beer Vomit
11. Iron and Wine
12. Amy Winehouse

13 ROCKERS TALK ABOUT BOOZE

1. "You know you're an alcoholic when you misplace a decade." (Paul Williams, *The Harder They Fall*)

2. "I like to say I only got drunk once—for thirty years." (Joe Walsh, *Rolling Stone*, Aug. 26, 2006)

3. "I've had a few times of being very drunk with sex where I did things I wouldn't have normally done, like not wear a condom. That was disturbing! That was much more disturbing than if I had not been able to perform. I only had that happen the one time. Waking up the next day, I couldn't believe I did it." (Andrew W.K., *NME*, Aug. 20, 2010)

4. "There are a lot of times when we don't get any sleep. For instance, when you're on the bus, the only way to sleep in the bus, at least for me, is to just get bombed and pass out. So, then you wake up like three hours later on a sugar high from all the liquor." (Duff McKagan, *Circus*, Sept. 1989)

5. "Somebody said to me one time, 'Ozzy I've heard you bellyaching, imagine for once if you were the sober one and you go home and your wife is lying in a puddle of her own urine with her (expletive) hanging on the floor, do you think you'd stay around?' When someone put it that way to me I thought (expletive), I'm lucky to have a wife. Men are very selfish in a lot of ways." (Ozzy Osborne, the *Republican*, Sept. 30, 2010)

6. "When you're drinking warm Coca-Cola and your accountants and managers and booking agents are walking around with these nice glasses with nice red juice in it, you say, 'Hey, that doesn't look like what I've been drinking in the dressing room. What's that? I'm not going onstage unless I get to have what you have.'" (Maynard James Keenan, *Wine Spectator*, Nov. 2, 2006)

7. "Montrachets are great but I'm more of a Bâtard-Montrachet kind of guy." (Sammy "Cabo Wabo" Hagar, GoodFoodRevolution.com, Feb. 11, 2010)

8. "The drinking was just—it was an accepted escape. And it became more of the drinking, the drugging, the womanizing…all of that stuff. It eventually just took over. Just like any addiction." (Metallica's James Hetfield, Fox TV interview, 2009)

9. "There's a school of thought that [William] Burroughs talks about where each time you withdraw from drugs your cells die and when you come off the drugs they regenerate and there's this constant dying and being brought back to life that's a constant part of a junkie's experience and that keeps you looking young. Although Burroughs looked like shit. [*Laughs.*] But drinking doesn't do that; drinking just hits you like a freight train and there's no way around it." (Nick Cave, Spinner.com, Oct. 23, 2008)

10. "I drink all day, every day." (Shane MacGowan in a post-show interview with Dutch television)

11. "[B]efore I started drinking, I always thought of Heineken as a step above. It's taken a while to get with a beer sponsor, but it's certainly something we can endorse. We are whatever the opposite of a beer snob is. It's like, 'Hey, drink this one.' Okay, fine. There isn't a ton of discrimination." (the Hold Steady's Craig Finn, *Broward–Palm Beach New Times*, May 20, 2010)

12. "I'm happy to be sober. Happy to be alive. I found myself in some places I can't believe I made it out of alive…. People with guns. People with gunshot wounds. People with heavy drug problems. People who carried guns everywhere they went, always had a gun. You live like that…you attract lower company." (Tom Waits, the *Observer*, Oct. 29, 2006)

13. "Herb is the healing of a nation, alcohol is the destruction." (Bob Marley)

12 SONGS ABOUT COCKTAILS (RECIPES INCLUDED!)

1. "Martini," Incubus

In a cocktail shaker or large glass filled with about six ice cubes, pour in 2.5 oz gin and .25 oz dry vermouth. Stir or shake, according to preference, and strain into chilled martini glass. Drop one green olive into bottom of glass or dress with a lemon-peel twist—your choice.

2. "Brass Monkey," Beastie Boys

Twist the cap off a bottle of Olde English (malt liquor) and chug until it's empty down to the label. Then pour in a small container of orange juice and swirl gently. (Warning: Shaking too vigorously may cause contents to explode and you'll lose precious nectar.) Enjoy from bottle. Straw optional. Burp, almost inevitable.

3. "Rum and Coca-Cola," the Andrews Sisters

Throw some ice cubes into a highball glass, almost filling it. Pour in 2 oz light rum and 5 oz Coca-Cola. Stir, garnish with lemon wedge, and take a sip. Adjust amounts accordingly.

4. "One Mint Julep," Ray Charles

Muddle four fresh mint leaves with 1 tsp powdered sugar, and 2 tsp water in a Tom Collins glass. Fill the glass with shaved or crushed ice and pour 2.5 oz bourbon over it. Stir. Garnish with a mint sprig and serve with straw.

5. "Moonlight Cocktail," Ames Brothers

Pour 2.5 oz top-shelf gin, .5 oz Cointreau, .5 oz crème de violette, and .5 oz fresh lime juice into a cocktail shaker that's two-thirds filled with ice. Shake for approximately 15 seconds and strain into a chilled champagne flute.

6. "Cuba Libre," Xavier Cugat

Drop four or five ice cubes into a highball glass. Add 1.5 oz rum (dark or light, depending on your preference), the juice of half a lime, and fill to the top with Coca-Cola. Garnish with lime wedge.

7. "Margaritaville," Jimmy Buffett

If you like your margaritas with salt, moisten the rim of the glass and dip in a plate of the stuff. Otherwise, just fill the glass with ice, dump in 1.5 oz of tequila *blanco* (100 percent agave, please—not the cheap crap, or you're just going to get a hangover), 1 oz freshly squeezed lime juice, and .5 oz Cointreau (not that nasty triple sec). Stir, drink. Start over.

8. "Brandy Alexander," Feist

The beverage of choice for grannies everywhere is made by carefully combining 1.5 oz brandy, 1 oz dark crème de cacao, and 1 oz half-and-half into a shaker that's half-full of ice. Shake well, strain into a cocktail glass, garnish with a pinch of nutmeg, and sip in front of your stories.

9. "Escape (the Piña Colada Song)," Rupert Holmes

Take 1.5 oz light rum, 2 oz cream of coconut, and 2 oz pineapple juice and combine in a blender with a cup of ice. Blend until smooth and pour into a Tom Collins glass. Garnish with pineapple and/or cherry and/or cute little paper umbrella. Best enjoyed not caught in the rain.

10. "Highballs," Guttermouth

A highball is basically any spirit served with a carbonated beverage over ice. So it could be as ghetto as rotgut and Sprite or as high-falutin' as a single-malt with artisanal sparkling water. It is always served in a highball glass, so if you mix it in an old-fashioned glass, it turns into a lowball, and nobody wants that. The trick is to add the ingredients (1 oz whiskey, 5 oz cold ginger ale) slowly, one at a time and don't stir too much or you'll flatten the bubbly ingredient. Garnish with a twist of lemon peel.

11. "Tequila Sunrise," Cypress Hill

If you're a member of Cypress Hill, before you do anything else, you light a fat blunt. Then you fill a glass halfway with ice. Exhale into the glass for a little smoky flavor. Add 2 oz gold tequila and 4 oz fresh orange juice. Put a flat-handled spoon into the glass and add .75 oz grenadine, allowing it to run down the spoon, so it sinks to the bottom of the glass, giving it that "sunrise" look. Garnish with maraschino cherry, an orange slice, and one of those little plastic monkeys. (Monkey is *not* optional.) Try to hold off drinking until you see the grenadine start to rise and spread through the rest of the beverage.

12. "Gin and Tonic Blues," Reverend Horton Heat

The good reverend and his boys have songs about pretty much every intoxicant under the sun, but in this one they pay tribute to that old standby, the G and T. To make a good one, you need to start with quality ingredients. Meaning, none of that store-brand gin. Pick up Tanqueray or Hendricks and pour 2 oz into a highball glass, filled almost to the top with ice. Then fill the remainder with good tonic water and garnish with a wedge of lime.

12 SONGS ABOUT WINE

1. "Ripple," Grateful Dead
2. "Red, Red, Wine," UB40
3. "Wine," the Raveonettes
4. "Black Fingernails, Red Wine," Eskimo Joe
5. "Night Train," Guns N' Roses
6. "Box Wine," Courtney Jaye
7. "Spill the Wine," Eric Burdon and War
8. "Wine," Supervolcano
9. "Strawberry Wine," Ryan Adams
10. "Summer Wine," Nancy Sinatra and Lee Hazlewood

11. "The Days of Wine and Roses," Dream Syndicate
12. "God of Wine," Third Eye Blind

12 PRODUCT-PLACEMENT SONGS

1. "Pass the Courvoisier," Busta Rhymes
2. "Grey Goose," Allstar Cashville Prince featuring Yo Gotti and Lil Wayne
3. "Ten Rounds with Jose Cuervo," Tracy Byrd
4. "Patrón," Sean Garrett featuring Pharrell
5. "Mad Dog 20/20," Roach Motel
6. "Colt 45," Afroman
7. "I'm So Gone (Patrón)," Chamillionaire featuring Bobby Valentino
8. "Hennessey," 2Pac and Obie Trice
9. "Stoli," Penelope Houston
10. "Jack Daniel's and Pizza," Carnivore (Don't listen to it!)
11. "Sue Jack Daniels," Reverend Horton Heat
12. "Ciroc," Messy Marv

12 (NOT 99) SONGS ABOUT BEER

1. "I Wish You Were a Beer," Cycle Sluts from Hell
2. "Beer Muscles," Scatterbrain
3. "Who Spilt My Beer?" the Adicts
4. "Beer Beer Beer!," Flogging Molly
5. "Beer Thirty," Brooks and Dunn
6. "Beer," Asylum Street Spankers
7. "Beer Goggles," Smashmouth
8. "Beer for Breakfast," the Replacements
9. "I Believe I'll Have Another Beer," Fear
10. "Rednecks, White Socks and Blue Ribbon Beer," Johnny Russell
11. "Beercan," Beck
12. "Two Pints of Lager and a Packet of Crisps Please," Splodgenessabounds

12 SONGS ABOUT TEQUILA

1. "Tequila," the Ventures
2. "Tequila Sundae," Urge Overkill
3. "Holiday in Spain," Counting Crows
4. "Pussy and Patron," Gucci Mane
5. "Tequila Makes Her Clothes Fall Off," Joe Nichols
6. "Tequila Sunrise," Eagles
7. "Tattoos and Tequila," Vince Neil
8. "Mas Tequila," Sammy Hagar and the Waboritas
9. "Tequila Sheila," Bobby Bare
10. "Jesus and Tequila," the Minutemen
11. "Mexican Moon," Concrete Blonde
12. "Tequila," the Pretenders

12 SONGS ABOUT WHISKEY

1. "Whiskey Drinkin' Woman," Nazareth
2. "Whiskey Bent and Hell Bound," Hank Williams, Jr.
3. "Women Without Whiskey," Drive-By Truckers
4. "Whiskey, You're the Devil," the Clancy Brothers
5. "Poison Whiskey," Lynyrd Skynyrd
6. "Whiskey Tango," Tanya Donnelly
7. "Alabama Song (Whiskey Bar)," The Doors
8. "Irish Whiskey," Cherry Poppin' Daddies
9. "Nancy Whiskey," Shane MacGowan and the Popes
10. "Captain Jack," Billy Joel
11. "Whiskey," the Gits
12. "Streams of Whiskey," the Pogues

12 SONGS ABOUT GIN

1. "Gin 'n' Juice," Snoop Dogg
2. "Cold Gin," Kiss
3. "Love Is Like a Bottle of Gin," Magnetic Fields
4. "Gin-Soaked Boy," Divine Comedy/Tom Waits
5. "Gin House Blues," Nina Simone
6. "Misery and Gin," Merle Haggard
7. "Tanqueray," Johnny Johnson
8. "Gin and Tonic Blues," Reverend Horton Heat
9. "Gin," Tiger Lillies
10. "Sloe Gin," Joe Bonamassa
11. "One Mo' Gin," D'Angelo
12. "Gin and Milk," Dirty Pretty Things

12 SONGS ABOUT CHAMPAGNE

1. "Champagne Supernova," Oasis
2. "Shampain," Marina and the Diamonds
3. "Champagne Life," Ne-Yo
4. "Champagne (Goodandevil mix)," Amanda Lepore
5. "Champagne for My Real Friends, Real Pain for My Sham Friends," Fall Out Boy
6. "Pop Champagne," Jim Jones and Ron Browz
7. "Champagne Taste," Eartha Kitt
8. "Champagne," Cavo
9. "Poppin' Champagne," All Time Low
10. "Champagne, Chronik Nightcap," Solange and Lil Wayne
11. "Champagne Bubble Bath," H Town
12. "Drinkin' Champagne," Willie Nelson

HONORABLE MENTION

"No Sex in the Champagne Room," Chris Rock (Not a song, but funny!)

EPILOGUE: WHEN SEX MEETS DRUGS

ALL MIXED UP

13

ANDREW W.K.'S 8 ROOKIE PARTY-THROWER MISTAKES

8. Carpets and Rugs

Even though carpets cushion the foot and rugs offer a beautiful way to decorate, these fibrous floor blankets quickly bunch up when people try to dance, and become stinking sponges for spilled savories and broken beverage bottles. Wood, concrete, or tile floors are far better—they're easier to clean, to dance upon, and to lick. Or just party on the natural grounds of the dirty Earth—the soil is made for your pleasure.

7. Mrs. Cavendish

I'm not saying she isn't a wonderful lady, but Mrs. Cavendish doesn't belong at our parties. In case you hadn't heard, she once punched my mom in the throat—that's totally unacceptable. My mom didn't deserve it at all. She had politely requested that Mrs. Cavendish stop climbing around in our kitchen cabinets. Instead of apologizing and cleaning up the mess, Mrs. Cavendish popped my mom right in the jugular with her fat fist. As a result, Mrs. Cavendish is no longer welcome at my parties, and I recommend you ban her from your celebrations too.

6. Too Many Dogs or Cats

I love cats. They have soft paws, funny claws, and fresh faces. They also pounce on bugs and play with them. I once saw a cat press down on a bug's body until it was completely flat. I love dogs too. They have smiling faces, wagging tails, and nice fluffy flanks for petting, patting, and stroking. However, too many of these beasts are crazed with foam rabies—and that can turn a party into the petting zoo from hell. Our festivities are no place for a killer kennel club—too much cat hair in your mouth starts to get irritating after a while. And too many dogs mean too much barking, barfing, and barging into the private areas between the legs of a young person. Keep them in cages or keep them outside, but don't let those hounds and catties run wild and take over your celebration. This party is for humans and cats and dogs, in that order. If the animals take control, you may never get it back.

5. Don't Invite Girls

About three years ago I went into the garage at a party and realized that the host didn't invite any girls. It wasn't just this one time. I realized he didn't invite girls to any of his parties. My first hunch was that he didn't like girls at all, but I had seen him enjoying the female form and figure in print and film—maybe he was just too afraid to talk to them. Either way, having a woman, girl, babe, or any other sort of female around helps round out the curve of the human spirit. Just being able to talk to a girl is a healthy release. Don't be the guy who didn't invite girls. Keep yourself (and your pals) in good health—invite gals!

4. Forget to Promote

You also don't want to be the guy who forgot to promote. People can't come to a party if they're not aware of the party. People can't show up and prance if they never heard there was a dance. It's so important to spread the word and promote the party that I can't overstress it enough. Your party exists! And the world deserves to hear about it! Print up some postcards and flyers. Talk about it on the telephone. Call up local businesses and encourage them to tell their employees about the event. Offer crushed-ice discounts, daily double promo points, and cash-back incentives. Anything that helps get the excitement going. Remember, you can't promote gallons of milk at a deep discount without an official announcement party—and iced rice–cream cups.

3. No Visible Trash Cans

This is a simple warning: If people can't see your trash cans, they'll use your entire place as a giant trash can.

2. No Towels in the Bathroom

Bathroom towels aren't just for drying your hands after washing. They're also for cleaning up filth and mess. There's nothing worse than accidentally urinating all over your hands, all over the toilet seat, all over the floor, walls, and door, only to realize there are no towels. Even worse is a letting out a whole bunch of strong diarrhea—that stuff is thick and sticky and smells so bad. Without any towels to wipe up the mess, the best you can do is dab at it with a ball of toilet paper. But toilet paper is so thin and made to dissolve in liquid, so it just turns to a slimy pulp the second it touches the urine or diarrhea. It's just a mess.

I. Telling People How to Party

Out of all the party mistakes I've listed here, the biggest one by far is telling other people how they should party. Even the most intelligent, freedom-loving, open-minded person will sometimes get it into their head that they know best, and that everyone should do the same stuff they do—that's a huge and terrible mistake. Everyone is different, and everyone has different ideas of what "fun" is. True partying is allowing everyone to have their own idea of fun, and to let each person celebrate the way that makes them happy. As long as one person's idea of fun doesn't interfere with another person's, then all their various tastes are valid. We all want to experience joy—joy is our common ground—how we get to that state of joy will vary from person to person, place to place, day to day. We're all individuals bound together by a shared purpose—to enjoy our lives before we die. Everything else is just a bunch of bullshit. PARTY HARD!

Andrew W.K. is the KING OF PARTYING, infamous for his bloody nose, famous for his high-life attitude, beloved for his songs like "PARTY HARD" and "YOU WILL REMEMBER TONIGHT." Andrew's true will is to use all forms of entertainment to create feelings of pure joy, fun, love, freedom, and possibility.

12 SONGS ABOUT THE FATAL COMBINATION OF LOVE AND LIQUOR

1. "She Only Likes Me When She's Drunk," the Stereos
2. "Too Drunk to Fuck," Dead Kennedys
3. "Don't Come Home A-Drinkin'," Loretta Lynn
4. "That Woman's Got Me Drinkin'," Shane MacGowan and the Popes
5. "Drinkin' and Dialin," Darius Rucker
6. "I Can't Stand Up for Falling Down," Elvis Costello
7. "You Only Tell Me You Love Me When You're Drunk," Pet Shop Boys
8. "Warm Beer, Cold Women," Tom Waits
9. "Why Don't We Get Drunk and Screw," Jimmy Buffett
10. "You Look Better When I'm Drunk," White Tie Affair
11. "Hurricane Drunk,"" Florence and the Machine
12. "Drunk Girls," LCD Soundsystem

BOB BERT'S TOP 5 SONGS ABOUT SEX OR DRUGS THAT YOU MAY NOT HAVE REALIZED WERE ABOUT SEX OR DRUGS

I. "Straight Shooter," the Mamas and the Papas

I used to sing this song as a youngster in my older sister's bedroom. Recently, I was talking about it to an ex-addict friend who said, "That's such a drug song." Listening back, it was quite obvious: "Baby are you holding, holding anything but me, cause I'm a real straight shooter if you know what I mean." Written by Papa John Phillips, whose life story makes Keith Richards' *Life* read like a nursery rhyme.

2. "Dirty Back Road," the B-52s

My favorite B-52s song and the best song about anal sex ever written. "Like a road you ride me!"

3. "Coming Down Again," the Rolling Stones

Great song sung by Keith on the *Goats Head Soup* album. With a line like "Stuck my tongue in someone else's pile," it could be about sex or drugs but I'm pretty sure it's about drugs.

4. "I Need Lunch," Dead Boys

We're not talking about PB&J sandwiches here, we're talking Lydia Lunch who, as a teenager ravaging the streets of NYC, got to know every member of the band intimately. "Girl I don't really want to dance, girl I just wanna get in your pants."

5. "Do Me In Once and I'll Be Sad, Do Me In Twice and I'll Know Better (Circular Circulation)," the GTO's

I'm pretty sure this song is about female masturbation. "This circular circulation, I circle continuously, to prepare myself for memories and have a talk with me."

BOB BERT'S TOP 5 EXTREMELY OBVIOUS SONGS ABOUT SEX OR DRUGS

1. "Heroin," the Velvet Underground
"It's my wife and it's my life."

2. "Love Comes in Spurts," Richard Hell and the Voidoids
"Oh no, it hurts!"

3. "Needle and Spoon," Savoy Brown
"Well I sleep with the sun and I rise with the moon, but I feel alright with my needle and spoon."

4. "Too Much Junkie Business," the Heartbreakers
"Climbing up the walls, shot some on my balls."

5. "If You Don't Want to Fuck Me, Baby Fuck Off," Jayne County
Nothing like being direct, I always say.

In addition to being a talented visual artist, Bob Bert has played drums for Sonic Youth, Pussy Galore, Bewitched, Action Swingers, Chrome Cranks, Knoxville Girls, and Int'l Shades, to name but a few. In 1995, he and his wife, Linda Wolfe, began publishing BB Gun (BBGun. org), where they ran interviews with such luminaries as Nancy Sinatra, Vincent Gallo, James Chance, Genesis Breyer P-Orridge, Cynthia Plaster Caster, Lydia Lunch, and Richard Hell, among many others. The pair is currently compiling their archives for *BB Gun*, the book.

RAY GANGE'S TOP 10 SEX, DRUGS, AND ROCK 'N' ROLL MOVIES

1. *Easy Rider*
An iconoclastic movie with an amazing soundtrack, it set the tone for everything that followed. Also, directed by a guy that was out of his mind—Dennis Hopper.

2. *Performance*
A mind-blowing movie with everything you could want—beautiful girls, drugs, gangsters, and *the* rock star (Mick Jagger). The soundtrack features the excellent "Memo from Turner."

3. *Spinal Tap*
You cannot discuss movies with a rock 'n' roll theme without putting this somewhere near the top. Sex and drugs may not feature, but the effects of sex and drugs are more than evident. One of the greatest comedies *ever*!

4. *Goodfellas*
Probably the best gangster movie of all time, with one of the best soundtracks too. Drugs and '70s Stones songs aplenty…do movies get better than this?

5. *Drugstore Cowboy*
It sums up the nihilistic self-destructive poetry of living life with a sex, drugs, and rock 'n' roll attitude without the trappings (or money) of a rock 'n' roll lifestyle.

6. *End of the Century*
The Ramones are responsible for almost all I hold dear. Would punk have happened without the Ramones? Possibly, but that ain't the way it happened. To misquote a line from Dee Dee's "Chinese Rocks," they shoulda been rich, but they were just digging a Chinese ditch. Sex—girlfriends were stolen from each other. Drugs—how many bands celebrated the gutter life of glue sniffing like the Ramones. They gave rock 'n' roll a new identity. God bless the Ramones!

7. *The Decline of Western Civilization 2: The Metal Years*

Decline 2 was directed by an ex-girlfriend of mine, Penelope Spheeris (who owes me a writing credit for *Suburbia*, by the way). The easiest way to explain this movie is that the bands in this movie appear to believe that Spinal Tap is a template for living. Hilarity and pathos abound in this documentary; a truly squirm-in-your-seat experience as you watch one shaggy-haired dude after another outdo each other in the *Beavis and Butthead* tribute show.

8. *Sid & Nancy*

The *Romeo and Juliet* of punk, so Shakespearean in its reality you'd never have made this up—sex and drugs and rock 'n' roll and murder. The London boy and the girl from NYC; the two homes of punk rock. Were it not for the fact that these were real people, you'd have to say that this story ends just like it should.

9. *Cocksucker Blues*

Hard to find and, not surprisingly, rarely seen. Get a copy of this by hook or by crook (on which note, someone stole mine). Seventies rock star excess and everything you could hope to see. Jagger's lawyers must've been busting blood vessels to stop this seeing the light of day

10. *Head*

Turn on, tune in, drop onto your ass, and figure out how this ever managed to get made. The names behind this are now stellar, and it serves at as a great middle-finger salute to everyone who was putting the Monkees down for being bubblegum airheads. Late-night viewing at its finest

Ray Gange starred in the Clash movie *Rude Boy* [which should've been on this list, but he's too modest—ed.] and lives in London and Hastings, UK, and is a painter and punk 'n' roll DJ.

STEVEN BLUSH'S 11 MOST FUCKED-UP SONGS OF AMERICAN HARDCORE

All-American hardcore music was fucked up in way or another. That was the whole point! The songs had no verse-chorus harmony, the lyrics bordered on obscene. It was radio unfriendly. Having said that, here's some of that insane era's most disturbing material that only the bravest DJs dare play, risking getting thrown off the air or shut down by the FCC.

1. "Crippled Children Suck," Meatmen
Menacing Motown front man Tesco Vee taught little kids by day and shoved mics up his ass by night.

2. "Cops for Fertilizer," Crucifucks
Must've been something in the Michigan water. Every cop in America back then knew of Doc Dart's crew.

3. "How Much Art Can You Take?," SS Decontrol
Boston HC's anthem of anti-intellectualism—as in "how many faggy new wave types can you deal with?"

4. "Jesus Entering from the Rear," Feederz
Phoenix freak singer and hoaxer Frank Discussion's paean to sacrilege and sodomy still shocks and rocks.

5. "Skinheads Smoke Dope," Fang
Skinhead singer Sammy smoked so much dope he killed his girlfriend! On parole, he's back with the band!

6. "Killing Children," Killing Children
Columbus, Indiana's contribution to HC—ninety-five seconds of mayhem—must've killed 'em in the Corn Belt!

7. "Love in Your Mouth," Nig-Heist
Black Flag's long-haired burnout roadies bummed out punkers with every imaginable type of crass behavior.

8. "My Woman from Sodom," Mentors

El Duce's disgusting odes to rape and misogyny were first to get singled out by Tipper Gore's PMRC witch hunt.

9. "Get Off the Air," Angry Samoans

Great song, but probably not the best career move to out KROQ DJ Rodney Bingenheimer back in 1980.

10. "My Dad's a Fuckin' Alcoholic," Frantix

A slow, creepy romp of suburban Denver angst and alienation. Still one of the best annoying songs ever.

11. "Alcohol," Gang Green

Disturbing lyrics include "I'd rather drink than fuck" and "You got the beer, we got the time / You got the coke, gimme a line!"

Steven Blush has written three books on the subject of rock: *American Hardcore* (Feral House, 2001), a history of the early-'80s hardcore punk scene; *American Hair Metal* (Feral House, 2006), a visual tribute to big-haired rockers; and *.45 Dangerous Minds* (Creation, 2005), a collection of interviews with pop culture's most notorious inhabitants. His writing has appeared in more than twenty-five publications, including *Spin, Details, Interview, the Village Voice*, and the *Times* of London. For over fifteen years he published the cult magazine *Seconds*, and he still serves as contributing editor for *Paper*. He worked for many years as a New York club DJ/promoter, noted for his "Röck Cändy" parties at Don Hill's and sound design for fashion designer Stephen Sprouse. Blush wrote and produced the *American Hardcore* documentary film (Sony Picture Classics, 2006), and followed that with an expanded and revised second edition of the *American Hardcore* book (Feral House, 2010).

ERIC DAVIDSON'S 5 MOST STRANGELY DISGUSTING *THINGS I EVER HEARD AT A GIG AFTER-PARTY*

1. "I like your bald head. I'd like to rub my pussy on it."
2. "You fuckin' pissed on this beer tap?! When?" (As he proceeded to fill his cup.)
3. "Just because it dropped on the toilet seat doesn't mean I can't snort it, ya dummy!"
4. "Those little egg salad sandwiches you guys just ate—I jerked off in one of them."
5. "That guy tried to fuck my girlfriend the last time he was in town! I wonder if he did?"

ERIC DAVIDSON'S 5 BEST IN-VAN TIME-SAVING TOUR HABITS OF, UM, HUMBLE PUNK ROCK BANDS

1. When choosing snacks, get Pringles. The can is large enough to piss in later. (Warning: It may leak. Also, I don't think Pringles have Olestra in them anymore. Whew.)

2. Wash it down with two-liter bottles of soda. (see #1)

3. If in a relatively modern minivan, wrap shoulder seat belt around right arm; slide open side door; lean out; and pee with the trail of the wind.

4. Bananas, bananas, bananas.

5. Coffee is a fickle lover. Use wisely.

9 LAME ROCK STAR TWEETS

Not only has Twitter taken the mystery out of celebrity, it's also acting as a crush crusher. Even worse than John Cusack's atrocious spelling are Slash's tweets about scented candles. Shouldn't he be talking about banging groupies, or at the very least—guitars? Here are eight rockers who should step away from the computer.

1. @NikkiSixx
Has anybody else ever had people that they are following just disappear and then reappear on twitter? It used to happen on myspace to me . . .

2. @MrTommyLand (Tommy Lee)
Is it wrong that my girl and I give each other full poop reports when we exit the bathroom?

4. @bretmichaels
RT @bretmichaels they don't sell your snapple in Canada.

5. @freddurst
"There's a good feeling to be had from sharing" —Linus

6. @travisbarker
Just took my little girl to ballet. #KIDSARESORAD

7. @Mr.VinceNeil
Locked himself outta the house and now has to call a goddamn locksmith. #mylifesux

8. @Slash
Check out www.kaifragrance.com they make killer smelling candles, air freshners & other aromatic house stuff. They're amazing! Iii|;)'

9. @thisisrobthomas (Rob Thomas, Matchbox 20)
I do believe that PARENTHOOD is one of the best shows on tv.

10 NOTORIOUS ROCK HOTELS

Rock stars are notoriously destructive hotel guests. When they're not throwing television sets out the windows, they're burning holes into the mattress with forgotten joints, spilling wayward groupie fluids on the carpeting, and generally raising hell. The upside: rock stars are generally rich and can pay for the messes they make. Here are ten of the most notorious rock hotels of all time.

I. Chelsea Hotel (New York City)

Sid Vicious may or may not have killed Nancy Spungeon here. Leonard Cohen wrote a song about getting a blowie from Janis Joplin while her limo idled outside. Dee Dee Ramone lived here, as did Patti Smith and Bob Dylan. The who-stayed-here list reads like a who's-who of rock 'n' roll—everyone from the Grateful Dead to the Libertines. Unfortunately, the recent years have not been kind to the family-owned Chelsea and due to infighting and squabbling this magnificent building is up for sale.

2. Chateau Marmont (Los Angeles)

Built in the late 1920s, this gorgeous hotel has withstood several earthquakes, John Belushi's overdose, and a long-term stay by Courtney Love. Love's stay culminated in her daughter filing an order of protection against her. There must be something in the water (or the bar) because Britney Spears also had a major freak-out here and was banned after she smeared her dinner all over her face instead of pushing it down her piehole, where it belonged.

3. St. Peter's Guest House (New Orleans)

This cheery pink French Quarter hotel is best known for being the spot where Johnny Thunders left this mortal coil on April 23, 1991. By the time the Heartbreaker's body was discovered in his ransacked room, rigor mortis had twisted his body into a *U*, though neighbor Willie DeVille assured the press Thunders had been found lying on the ground, guitar in hand. Later he admitted only to seeing a U-shaped body bag being dragged out of the hotel. It's said that Johnny still haunts the room 37 and to this day, his cause of death has never been determined.

4. Continental Hyatt House (Los Angeles)

Once it was affectionately dubbed the "Riot Hyatt"; now this Sunset Strip hotel is known as the Andaz West Hollywood. Keiths Richards and Moon both heaved televisions out the Hyatt's windows, and Led Zeppelin used to rent out the entire top floor—including the roof with the pool—when they were in town. Little Richard lived here and pretty much any band worth listening to (and their attending groupies) left its mark on the place.

5. Austin Motel (Austin, TX)

Featuring a vintage neon sign that very much resembles an erect penis and scrotum, the Austin is kitschy, quaint, and centrally located for bands playing SXSW or anywhere else in the music-friendly city. Because it lacks the amenities big rock stars crave these days, you won't find your Coldplayers lingering by the pool (thank God), but you might just run into that fine bass player you were scoping at the Continental the night before.

6. The Columbia Hotel (London)

Back when they were just fledgling egomaniacs, Oasis stayed here and were eventually banned for—you guessed it—tossing televisions out the window. They had such fond memories of the place they even wrote the song "Columbia" about it. In fact, it was their first demo and gave the warring brothers a big leg up. More recently the Columbia has housed the fabulous Scissor Sisters, Killing Joke, and Iggy Pop.

7. Pavillon de la Reine (Paris)

This ivy-covered seventeenth-century Right Bank hotel doesn't attract the TV tossers but instead caters to more cerebral rock stars, such as the members of Radiohead; Madonna's conical-bra designer, Jean Paul Gaultier; and punk poetess Patti Smith, who stays here every time she's in Paris.

8. The Phoenix (San Francisco)

According to Red Hot Chili Pepper Anthony Kiedis, the Phoenix is "the most sexually, intellectually, and culturally stimulating hotel in San Francisco." Say what? There must be an element of truth there, because Joan Jett, Little Richard, Pearl Jam, the Killers, and the Shins have all slipped between the sheets here. Even the hotel's website admits it can be noisy, so bring your earplugs.

9. Ace Hotels (New York; Portland, OR; Palm Springs; and Seattle)

You're not going to run into Keef or Mick in the lift, but these hipster hot spots are packed with indie rockers on low-budget tours and people who look like indie rockers on low-budget tours. The NY location is especially star-heavy, having held performances by Nas, Q-Tip, and Casey Spooner in their bar and being home to *the* go-to restaurant in the neighborhood.

10. Swingos Celebrity Inn (Cleveland, OH)

Rock hotels aren't always the fanciest, and in the case of the notorious Swingos, this was definitely the case, with onetime Little Feat tour manager Gene Vano dubbing it "a dump but it had a great restaurant and every room had a theme, like French Provincial." In its day (it closed in 2009), Swingos was a temporary home for everyone from Frank Sinatra to President Jimmy Carter to Avril Lavigne. Elvis Presley was so fond of the place he turned it into base camp for his Midwest tour, gobbling up three entire floors.

8 ODD ROCK 'N' ROLL RIDERS

I. Fatboy Slim

"My rider is a bottle of vodka and a liter of orange juice, though at certain clubs there are other 'extras.' At one London club I get two E's and a gram of coke, on top of the vodka and orange. If there's only one person playing your venue, you can afford to spoil them." (*Spin*, Oct. 1998)

2. Lemmy Kilmister (Motörhead)

"[Lemmy] had a plaid bag with three books and a notepad. No change of clothes. His fucking rider was seven bottles of bourbon, eight bottles of vodka, two bottles of orange juice, and that's fucking it!" (Ozzy Osbourne, talking about Kilmister, *Rolling Stone*, Oct. 20, 2009)

3. AC/DC

- Three oxygen tanks with three masks that must be at the venue at load-in
- Two live potted trees, height according to ceiling

- One case of bottled Heineken (Note: no beer in dressing room prior to show.) Please stock beer in dressing room 15 minutes after AC/DC goes onstage.
- Small selection of candy bars (fun size)

(Excerpts from AC/DC's 2008 rider, courtesy of the Smoking Gun)

4. Jane's Addiction

According to BBC news, the band requested their dressing rooms have an "earthy, velvet/velour-type atmosphere." They also asked for washing machines and a room to jam in for two hours before going onstage—which had to have a "contemporary black leather atmosphere with potted indoor plants."

5. Beck

- Two packs of rice cakes
- One container of hummus
- Several bottles and cans of water
- Plain yogurt

(BBC News)

6. Rolling Stones

- One entire room devoted to the snooker table the band travels with
- Satellite TV hookup, capable of tuning into cricket matches
- Three Casablanca lily arrangements, three lily arrangements that also feature weeping eucalyptus and one lily and eucalyptus with white freesia. One small lavender plant (costing no more than $15), two wildflower arrangements, one long-stemmed white rose in vase with white freesia, and four dozen long-stemmed, dethorned white roses, wrapped in paper. (Smoking Gun)

7. Smokey Robinson

The Smokesman is most particular about the kind of bottled water he'll drink. Their rider reads (it's written in all caps, but I'll spare you): "Acceptable drinking water for the Smokey Robinson Organization is Naya, Desani [sic], Arrowhead, or Sparklettes." There's no boozin' for the SRO either. Other beverages include tea, Vernon's [sic] ginger ale, and pineapple or apple juice. Whereas the band gets assorted soft drinks, it's specified that the dancers only get diet versions. (The Smoking Gun)

8. The Village People

Though probably half of the Village People are fill-ins and the band isn't exactly packing arenas these days, these dudes still have needs. According to the blog Mental Floss, "The front page of their rider contains one stipulation: that all balances to the Village People be paid in 'CASH' (yes, it's in all caps)."

THE PMRC'S FILTHY 15

Once upon a time, in a world populated by disco-dancing women in shoulder pads and men wrapped in MC Hammer pants, four politically connected, uptight broads got together and decided that the devil's music was a grave danger to our nation's youth. To fight this scourge, they demanded that the record companies start labeling albums containing songs they deemed offensive. There were a series of alternately infuriating and entertaining hearings, with testimonies from the likes of Frank Zappa, Dee Snyder, and John Denver. The Recording Industry Association of America eventually agreed to the stickers and as a result, America is now home to only chaste, well-adjusted children. Phew!

Here were the first fifteen to spur the ladies into action.

1. "Darling Nikki," Prince

Nikki's habit of masturbating with periodicals in hotel lobbies was apparently more than the ladies could bear, so Prince made numero uno on their hit parade.

2. "Sugar Walls," Sheena Easton

Prince (naughty!) wrote this for the Scottish songstress using a pseudonym. "Sugar walls" are not part of a gingerbread house, but slang for what Oprah calls the "vajayjay."

3. "Eat Me Alive," Judas Priest

Blow jobs at gunpoint are filthy enough, but I imagine Tipper's top would've been blown twice if she'd known he was talking homo blowies.

4. "Strap On Robbie Baby," Vanity

Once a Prince protégé, then a Nikki Sixx fuck toy, now a born-again Christian, Vanity delivered this ode to pegging, which, predictably, did not go over big with the sphincter-locked ladies who lunched.

5. "Bastard," Mötley Crüe

This catchy little ditty about murdering a rapist raised hackles because of its extreme violence, though a few years later, GG Allin wrote lyrics that make these hair farmers sound like a bunch of Cub Scouts.

6. "Let Me Put My Love into You," AC/DC

Subtlety has never played a big part in the AC/DC songwriting process, so I suppose they should be commended for not naming the song "Let Me Put My Big Uncircumcised Cock into You." Yet still, even with the nice euphemism for ween, this upset the mommies.

7. "We're Not Gonna Take It," Twisted Sister

This song is about people sticking up for themselves, which seems pretty harmless until you consider the PMRC was trying to censor artists, so it makes sense they found it offensive.

8. "Dress You Up," Madonna

Madonna has written tons of filthy songs. This is not one of them. Unless by "dress you up in my love," she means, "let me slather my slick lady juices all over your body," in which case it's risqué.

9. "Animal (F**k like a Beast)," W.A.S.P.

Long before Trent Reznor was fucking you like an animal, W.A.S.P. was fucking you like the beasts they were. Have you ever seen a photo of these guys? That's simply truth in advertising.

10. "High 'n' Dry," Def Leppard

Along with sex and violence, drugs and booze were also on the white-lady blacklist. Yawn.

II. "Into the Coven," Mercyful Fate

Okay, besides sex, drugs, booze, and violence, the PMRC ladies also feared the devil. Now granted, *The Exorcist* showed us he's a scary dude, but banning all mentions smacks of religious intolerance. If you're going to ban the 'Fate, can we please also ban Amy Grant and Stryper?

I2. "Trashed," Black Sabbath

One good thing that came out of the PMRC debacle is that the resulting notoriety meant that Sabbath probably sold a few more copies of this stinker of an album.

I3. "In My House," Mary Jane Girls

Ignoring the fact that the ladies were named after OMG *marijuana*(!!), "In My House" was listed for bein' too sexxy.

I4. "Possessed," Venom

Again with the Satan hating! Tipper Gore, I'd sleep with one eye open if I were you.

I5. "She Bop," Cyndi Lauper

You can't get herpes from wanking and nobody ever got pregnant after a hot night of self-love action. Jilling off makes you smile and orgasms are good for your health. Yet despite all this evidence saying it's a good thing, the PMRC felt this song was disgusting. Maybe if they'd tried it, they would've liked it. And loosened up a bit.

HONORABLE MENTION

"Mother," Danzig

Though he wasn't mentioned during the hearings, friend to the devil (broad assumption, not fact) Glenn Danzig wrote what many consider to be his best song, critiquing and threatening the PMRC.

10 PLACES WHERE THE BOUNCING SOULS BEHAVE BADLY

We get three rooms a night on tour. Naturally, the pot smokers in the group end up together in their own room, and this is how the Pots were born. Then there are those few people smart enough to take it easy and rest up for the next show…maybe a little TV, then it's lights out. We call them the Sleeps.

Then there's our room—the Bads. The Bads are down for anything. It's the room where the after-party happens, or the one that's empty because its inhabitants are out all night mixing it up with the local riffraff, looking for trouble. The Bads are experts at finding trouble—we've been at it for over twenty years now. We just love a good hang with all our friends around the globe, so here's our list of top ten hangs:

I. Cafe the Minds (Amsterdam)
Amsterdam itself is a top hang and the Minds is a great little punk bar we always end up at after a night of being bad.

2. The Franken Bar (Berlin)
Located right across the street from our gig at SO36, this badass punk bar stays open late and there's always trouble to be found there. Say hi to Alice for us!

3. The Phoenix Hotel (San Francisco)
This is *the* rock 'n' roll hotel—a place of legendary all-nighters in the Bads' room. Jawing away about nothing all night with our friends from SF.

4. Bovine Sex Club (Toronto)
The best party in Canada. Great punk bar we always hit after the show. If we're lucky, they'll stay open extra late for us.

5. Punk Rock Bowling (Las Vegas)
Punk rock's biggest party of the year is hosted by our big brothers, Shawn and Mark Stern of Youth Brigade. The entire punk rock community descends on a casino for a weekend of music, bowling, and vices of every kind. It's a Bads national holiday.

6. New York City

When in the greatest city in the world, we like to bounce between two great punk bars in the East Village—Manitoba's (on Avenue B between Fifth and Sixth Streets), and the Double Down Saloon (on Avenue A between First and Second Streets). Handily enough, they're just within stumbling distance from each other.

7. Asbury Lanes (Asbury Park, NJ)

We've had more Bads times here, at our local watering hole on Fourth Avenue in Asbury Park, than anywhere else in the world. This is truly our home bar. Just two blocks from the ocean, and a short ride on a beach cruiser back home, hopefully before dawn.

8. Portland, OR

It's a great weird town where anything's possible. We dig the Jupiter Hotel, which has a great strip joint called Union Jacks practically next door. Also a killer breakfast at the Doug Fir, located right on the premises.

9. Los Angeles

Truly all the decadence anyone could ask for in a town. The bar names change, but with a little help from all our Bad friends, we always find a way to get weird in Hollywood. It starts at the show, continues onto a bar, and then on to a house or hotel room somewhere.

10. The NOFX tour bus

Formed in 1989 at a Knights of Columbus Hall in Bernardsville, NJ, the Bouncing Souls have been releasing quality punk rock for over two decades. True to their DIY roots, they've accomplished all this without major labels, corporate radio, MTV, or teen magazine pinups. FYI, this list was exhaustively researched and compiled by the two founding Bads, Pete and Bryan. Find out more at BouncingSouls.com.

THE HANGOVER

14

11 REHAB HALL-OF-FAMERS

Smug Ted Nugent was quoted in *Wall Street Journal* as saying, "Clean and sober for fifty-nine years, I am still rocking my brains out and approaching my six thousandth concert. Clean and sober is the real party." Well, Ted try convincing any of these peeps. None of them have ever been on *Celebrity Rehab* (yet), but I can certainly see at least one or two of them turning up in future seasons.

1. Courtney Love

Courtney has checked herself into rehabs, had cleaner-uppers come to her hotel room to help her kick, has been remanded into care, and was finally issued a restraining order by her own daughter. Yet she still maintains that addict mind-set where everything is everyone else's fault. She told *Clash* magazine that for a while she was completely broke after being "exploited" by hangers-on. "I wrote 'Never Go Hungry' all by my lonesome, in rehab, sitting there fucking in Orange County with a shit guitar and no pick."

2. Scott Weiland

When you type "Scott Weiland" and "rehab" into Google, you get over five hundred thousand hits immediately. The Velvet Revolver/Stone Temple Pilots front man has been on everyone's deathwatch list for years now. Whether he's remanded to rehab or walks in of his own volition, it never seems to stick.

3. Pete Doherty

The Libertines' front man is far more famous for his prodigious drug use and somehow convincing supermodel Kate Moss to schtup him than he ever was for being a musician. Pete goes to rehab as often as most of us gas up our car or get our hair cut. In 2004, he jetted off to Thailand to the Thamkrabok Monastery, where vomiting is one of the main treatment plans. Though they have a 70 percent success rate, the brutal routine was more than Doperty could handle, and he fled after three days.

4. Vince Neil

In 1984 Vince Neil's drunk driving killed Hanoi Rocks' drummer, Razzle. This might have scared a better man straight, but Vince kept on rocking, drinking, and drugging. He's been to rehab a bunch of times but insists it doesn't work, telling one reporter, "I don't think I'll ever have my drug problems licked. I still think about needles today. Thirty years later, I'll still look at a needle and go, 'F**k.' It's quite an itch. But I haven't thought about actually doing drugs in fifteen years. I kind of cringe at that idea. That was for the old days. But I have a drink once in a while. That doesn't hurt ya." Though it might kill your passenger.

5. Steven Tyler

Shouldn't the golden years of a multimillionaire be spent golfing or lounging by the pool? Not if you're Steven Tyler. After twelve years of sobriety, Tyler started snorting the sleep aid Lunestra (WTF?) and fell off the stage at an Aerosmith show. He didn't break his hip, but he did break his shoulder and needed a bunch of stitches. The incident scared the scrawny sixty-year-old straight (again) and he dutifully checked into a treatment center.

6. Whitney Houston

Will anyone ever forget Whitney regaling her pals with the tale of then-husband Bobby Brown reaching up into her opiate-clogged pooper to remove a lodged piece of dookie? "That's love—that's black love," she told her clearly horrified girlfriends. Then there was the time she insisted to Diane Sawyer that she'd never do crack because that was a "poor person's drug." (Freebase, however, is a completely other story.) Whit eventually ditched Bobby and hit rehab, but whether or not she's clean remains to be seen.

7. Stevie Nicks

The Gold Dust Woman was, in reality, much more fond of the white dust. By her estimates, she spent over a million bucks on the drug until a plastic surgeon told her that her nose was in grave danger of falling off if she kept up her habit (hence the rumor that her assistant used to blow it up her ass before gigs). She checked into Betty Ford and got that monkey off her back only to spend her forties addicted to the Klonopin that had helped her get over her coke jones.

8. Dave Mustaine

Getting kicked out of Metallica for being too much of a drunken, drug-addicted mess was quite a feat considering the nonsobriety of the rest of the band. But it didn't send Mustaine into treatment. That took a judge's order after a DUI. Estimates are that Mustaine was in and out of rehab at least fifteen times until he found God in the early aughts. In addition to playing music (but refusing to play on the same bill with any Satan-worshipping black metal bands!), he launched a line of coffees and teas with his wife.

9. Ron Wood

Though Keith Richards is probably the better-known Stone as far as drinking and drugging goes (I mean, the guy sent his blood out for cleaning!), with the exception of weed and booze, he's kept it in check for the past couple decades. Ron Wood, however, is quite a different story and has been back and forth from rehabs at least seven times. In 2008, he took a spectacular dive off the wagon, ditched his wife of twenty-three years for an eighteen-year-old Russian cocktail waitress whom he was subsequently arrested for battering.

10. Amy Winehouse

Sadly fitting that Amy Winehouse's biggest hit was "Rehab."

11. Eminem

He's named albums *Relapse* and *Recovery*. Getting fucked up and then not is a way of life for this guy. Though does anyone actually believe he checked into rehab for *Ambien*?

8 ROCK 'N' ROLL(ISH) CELEBRITY REHAB/SOBER HOUSE ALUMNI

Despite how beautifully he fills out a snug T-shirt, Dr. Drew has made a career out of capitalizing on other people's pain. He has sixteen-year-olds parading their pregnant bellies and loser baby daddys around on MTV, while pill poppers and sex addicts spill their guts poolside for a more sophisticated crowd on VH1. Whether or not his programs help anyone is up for debate, but here are seven of the more musically inclined *Celebrity Rehab/Sober House* alumni

1. Steven Adler (former Guns & Roses drummer, now founder/drummer, Adler's Appetite)

Drugs of choice: Heroin, cocaine, pot
Shows: *Celebrity Rehab*, season 2 and 5; *Sober House*, season 1
Update: Steven Adler was heavily intoxicated during a couple episodes of *Sober House* and was arrested, kicked out, and taken back into care. After the show ended, he was rearrested for skipping out on community service and remanded into (regular-people) rehab again. Setting off on a monthlong European tour, Adler rejoined Celebrity Rehab's fifth season, where he continued to act like an asshole.

2. Leif Garrett (former teen heartthrob/pop singer)

Drug of choice: Heroin
Show: *Celebrity Rehab*, season 4
Update: In January 2011, Garrett told the *Los Angeles Times* that while he had quit using heroin four days before filming began, producers pressured him to use on camera for the B roll. The producers of the show dispute this. Then, after completing the show, he broke his collarbone, was prescribed pain meds, and went back off the rails.

3. Tawny Kitaen (model, actress and star of the Whitesnake videos that launched a million cases of teen priapism)

Drugs of choice: Cocaine and various prescription drugs
Show: *Celebrity Rehab*, season 2

Update: Tawny was picked up for a DUI well after her stay with Dr. Drew but today seems healthy and happy in Newport Beach, where she helps at-risk women stay off the pills.

4. Mindy McCready (country singer)

Drugs of choice: Alcohol and various prescription drugs

Show: *Celebrity Rehab*, season 3

Update: McCready has had a rough life, peppered with domestic violence, suicide attempts, arrests, and a possible statutory rape situation with baseball star Roger Clemens. In 2010 she was briefly hospitalized after her mother (nice!) gave her some Darvocet. Like so many others, she also has a sex tape floating around out there.

5. Nikki McKibbin (*American Idol* finalist, vet of other reality shows)

Drugs of choice: Alcohol and cocaine

Shows: *Celebrity Rehab*, season 1; *Sober House*, season 1

Update: McKibbin initially blamed her descent into alcoholism and drug abuse on the harsh words of *American Idol* judge Simon Cowell, which might be funny had she not shared this story about the snippy Brit: "He told me that my eyes were beautiful and he wanted to take my eyeballs out of my head and put them on his nightstand so that he could look at them every night before he went to bed."

6. Shifty Shellshock (Crazy Town)

Drugs of choice: Any and all of 'em

Shows: *Celebrity Rehab*, seasons 1 & 2; *Sober House*, seasons 1 & 2

Update: Shifty was by far the biggest mess on any of Dr. Drew's shows. He smoked crack in front of the camera, cried, climbed the walls—you name the aberrant behavior, Shifty probably did it, on camera. These days he's performing and claims to be sober, though that claim is probably best taken with about an eight ball of salt.

7. Jessica Sierra (singer, former *American Idol* contestant)

Drugs of choice: Alcohol and cocaine

Shows: *Celebrity Rehab*, season 1

Update: Jessica relapsed after the show and was later remanded into a yearlong rehab. She also did jail time. Now single mom and sober, she's trying to relaunch her singing career.

8. Mike Starr (bassist, formerly in Alice in Chains)

Drugs of choice: Heroin, methadone, crystal meth, marijuana. (He was even filmed using drugs in a car with his dad.)

Shows: *Celebrity Rehab*, season 3; *Celebrity Rehab*, season 4 (just an appearance); *Sober House*, season 1. (He was in regular-people rehab over 30 times.)

Update: Along with other *CR* alums Mackenzie Phillips and Tom Sizemore, Starr appeared in season 4 to encourage that group to stay sober, and at that point he marked six months and seven days of sobriety. Unfortunately, Starr was the first post–Dr. Drew fatality, dying of a suspected drug overdose on March 8, 2011.

5 THINGS YOU GET AT FANCY CELEBRITY REHABS THAT YOU WON'T SEE AT YOURS

I. Equine-assisted therapy

Sierra Tuscon (where assorted members of Mötley Crüe allegedly did time) offers horsey time to their patients. According to their website, "Horses are typically nonjudgmental and have no expectations or motives."

2. Gourmet meals

You won't find those segmented trays full of gray mystery meat at Promises, Britney and Lindsay's rehab of choice. Instead, there are several gourmet chefs on staff who'll cater to your every dietary whim.

3. An ocean view, jacuzzis, pools, and tennis courts

Promises is also parked on a bluff in Malibu, allowing its clientele a cheerful peek at the Pacific. They "promise" that "a setting where sunny days, warm nights, and cool breezes are the norm can help remove some of the underlying issues associated with addiction."

4. Helicopter rides

Sundance, Utah, isn't just home to the famous film festival; it's also where you can find Cirque Lodge, a fancy-ass rehab that caters to the rich and famous. According to the Lodge, "You can enhance your experience in addiction treatment by participating in one of our helicopter tours, which transport you high into the beautiful surrounding mountains."

5. Spa services and complete privacy

Privé-Swiss is so plush they only accept three clients at a time. According to a story on MSNBC, "The program also offers twice-weekly massages, a gourmet cook, and opportunities for whale watching and shopping." However, Courtney Love has been a client, so you might want to think twice before you shell out.

ACKNOWLEDGMENTS

I'd like to thank my dearly departed mom for knowing I'd be a writer before I did. Kudos to my dad for grimacing quietly but keeping his mouth shut when I told him the title of this book. Thank you to his beautiful wife, Peg, for not batting an eyelash. My gorgeous sister, Sue, has always been massively supportive, and I'm sure my brothers, Jake and Mike, will be relieved that they're totally allowed to read this book (unlike the last one).

My man, Spyro, kept me supplied with Diet Coke and white wine, used every contact in his book to get me sources, and didn't freak out when I filled our entire apartment with books about music, drugs, and sex. I owe you big-time, bub.

High five to Mike Edison for saying yes to this mess, Cliff Mott for making it pretty, and to my agent, Bob Mecoy, for working out the details.

My well-connected and generous friends have been invaluable to this process. Mike Edison has been so patient, kind, smart, and understanding throughout the making of this book. Kurt B. Reighley knows everything there is to know about every kind of music and was nice enough to share. The brilliant Julie Mason pointed me toward Minor Threat's Steve Hansgen, while Kate Crane hooked me up with Kate Hiltz, who hooked me up with the Bouncing Souls and Cathy Mason. Lynn Von and Steve Pang introduced me to Sean Yseult, who graciously contributed. Bob Bert said yes, even though I hadn't seen him for years and the first thing I did was ask him a favor. Michael A. Gonzales made me laugh hysterically and gave me several soulful lists that I love. Zachary Lipez has been a sweetheart for many years and was kind enough to contribute. Eric Danville, who wrote *The Official Heavy Metal Book of Lists* and used to be my boss when we both slave-labored at *High Times*, was kind enough to write about Lenny Bruce. Illustrator extraordinaire Cliff Mott approached the mighty Joe McGinty, who was awesome enough to say yes. Diana G. hooked me up with the fearsome, funny, and charming black metal princess Sarah Jezebel Deva. Felice Ecker and Aleix Martinez of Girlie Action hooked me up with Princess Superstar—*gracias*! No sooner had I asked Steve Blush if he'd consider contributing than he shot back a list—damn, man! Thanks!

I'd also like to thank all the other amazing contributors, especially über-mensch Richard Manitoba, the hilarious Andrew WK, and the awe-inspiring Oderus Urungus. All the other people kind enough to contribute also have my undying gratitude: Pat Kiernan and Caitlin Drexler, Bouncing Souls, Cathy Mason, Bob Bert, Sean Yseult, Joe McGinty, Princess Superstar, Steve Hansgen, Michael Musto,

Amanda Hess, Ray Gange, Gay for Johnny Depp, Jiz Lee, the legendary Cynthia Plaster Caster, Norman Brannon, Eric Davidson, Rich Juzwiak, Theo Kogan, Mike McPadden, and finally, Coco! What a coup to win Coco!

I'm sure I forgot some people and for that I am sorry. It's all those drugs and sexy fluids coursing through my system. . . .

Printed in the United States
by Baker & Taylor Publisher Services